Encyclopedia of Spanish Period Furniture Designs

José Claret Rubira

 Sterling Publishing Co., Inc.   New York
Blandford Press   Dorset, England

Translated by Alice Hobson

Edited and designed by Barbara Busch

Library of Congress Cataloging in Publication Data

Claret Rubira, José.
   Encyclopedia of Spanish period furniture designs.

   Translation of: Muebles de estilo español.
   Includes index.
   1. Furniture—Spain.   I. Title.
NK2599.C5313   1984   749.26   84-8862
ISBN 0-8069-7902-X (pbk.)

CONTENTS

PUBLISHER'S PREFACE

Lovers of fine furniture, cabinetmakers, decorators, restorers, artists, stage designers—indeed, all who take pleasure in things of beauty will find something of value in this comprehensive source book on Spanish period furniture.

The illustrations on the following pages show Spanish furnishings from the Gothic period through the nineteenth century, offering a treasure house of ideas and details, in which can be found representatives of virtually every important period piece. The rich fabric of Spanish history embraced many cultural influences and they are all lavishly displayed here. Not only the furniture of palaces is to be seen, but also that of peasants. There are folk designs and motifs rarely found in books of this kind. The Moorish influence is seen in numerous pieces: in carved Mudejar benches and chests, in elaborate braziers and candle holders, in the exquisite tracery of wrought-iron.

The religious nature of the Spanish was another influence affecting the furniture. Stage designers and historians will delight in the church stalls and "confessional" armchairs. Some of the carvings that can be seen in the "church furniture" also influenced the carving of the home furnishings.

Spain also paid homage through its furnishings to other nations. Here are beds of Portuguese style, chairs of French influence and desks that might have been designed by Chippendale. But always there is an Hispanic flavor and charm.

All the magnificent massive pieces that most of us think of when we discuss Spanish furniture are shown, but there are many, many surprises—pieces of extreme delicacy and sometimes whimsy. The multiplicity of cultural influences combined to create a wealth of design that is unsurpassed in its variety.

PLATE 1

"Box" armchair, carved on both sides, from Alfabia (Majorca).

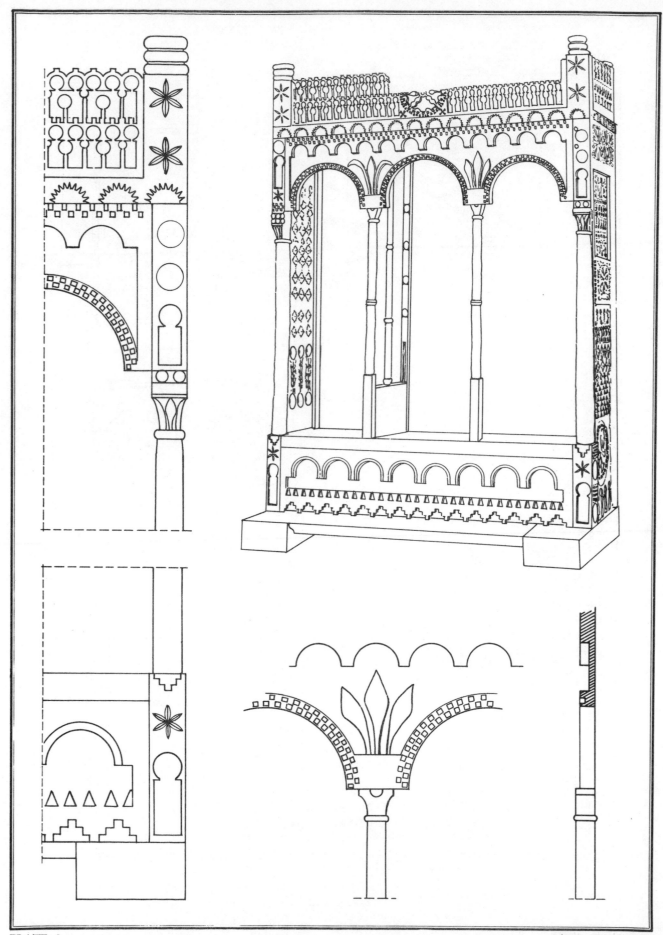

PLATE 2
Mudejar bench from church of Tahull.

Museum of Art of Catalonia, Barcelona

PLATE 3   LATE 14TH OR EARLY 15TH CENTURY

Faldistorium of King Martin I of Aragon, "The Humane" (1395–1410), which serves as a shrine for the monstrance in the Corpus Christi processions.

Treasury of the Cathedral, Barcelona

PLATE 4

LATE 14TH OR EARLY 15TH CENTURY

Small chest with carved decoration in the shape of "cloister windows."

PLATE 5
Carved writing desk with Gothic tracery.

15TH CENTURY

Concds de Casa-Puente collection, Madrid

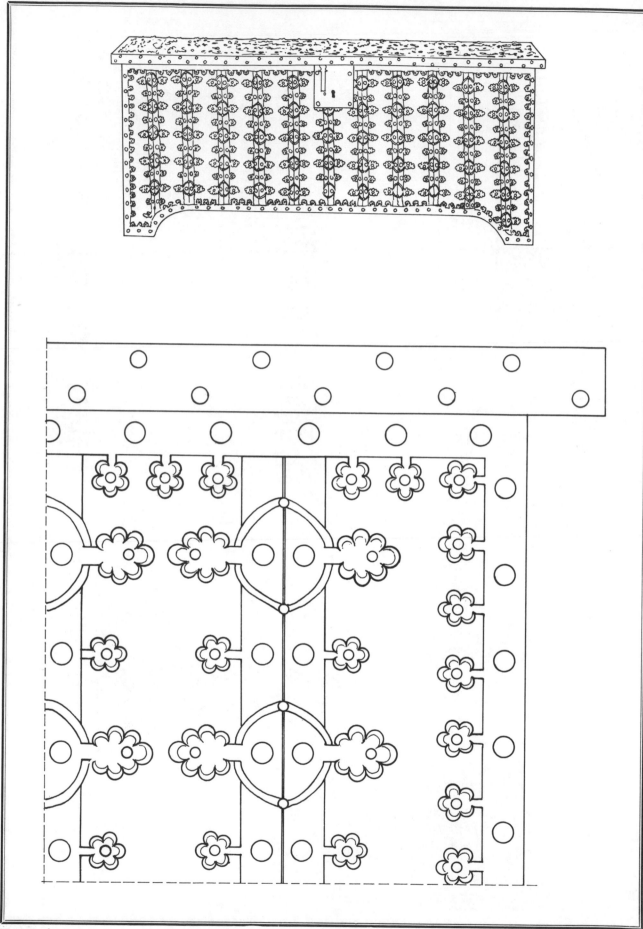

PLATE 6
Chest with wrought-iron trimming.

15TH CENTURY

PLATE 7
Gothic chest trimmed with wrought iron.

PLATE 8
Small carved chest with Gothic tracery.

15TH CENTURY

Valencia Don Juan Institute, Madrid

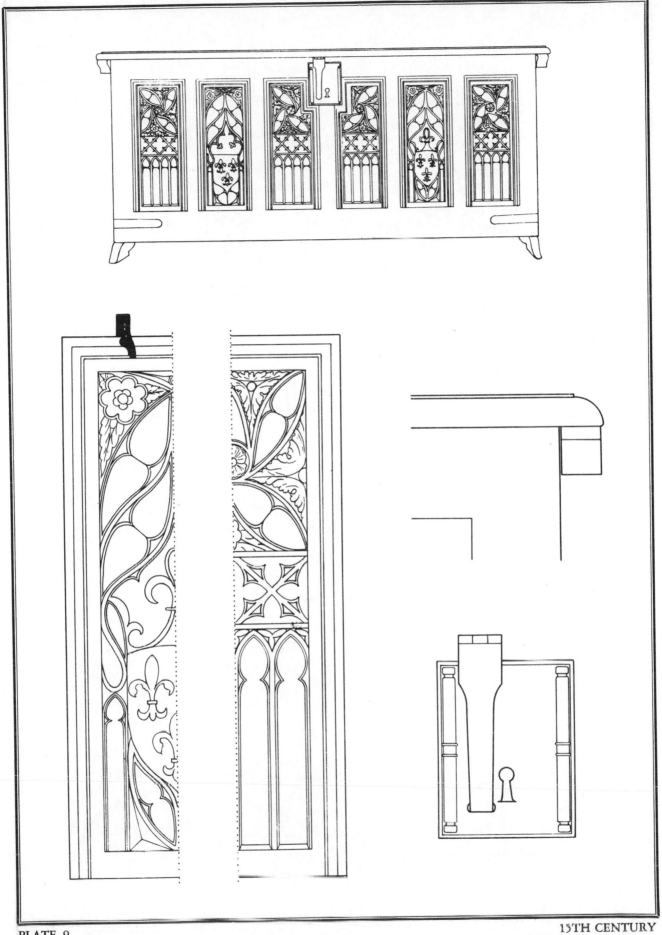

PLATE 9
Large carved chest with Gothic tracery.

National Archeological Museum, Madrid

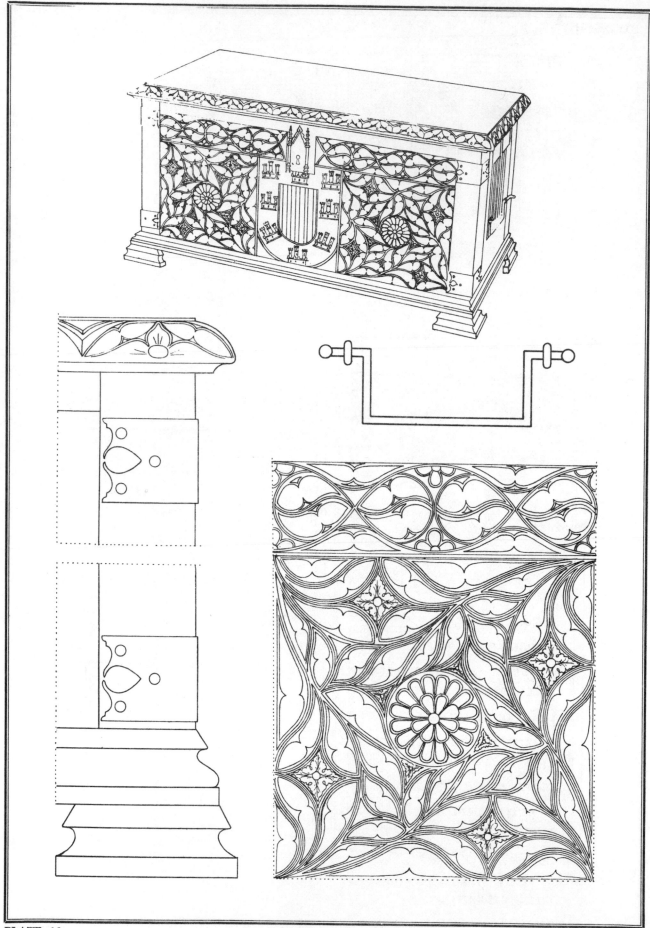

PLATE 10
Large carved chest with Gothic tracery and heraldic motif.

15TH CENTURY

Valencia Don Juan Institute, Madrid

PLATE 11
Large carved chest with Gothic tracery.

Lazaro Galdiano Museum, Madrid

PLATE 12
Small gothic chest with carved decoration.

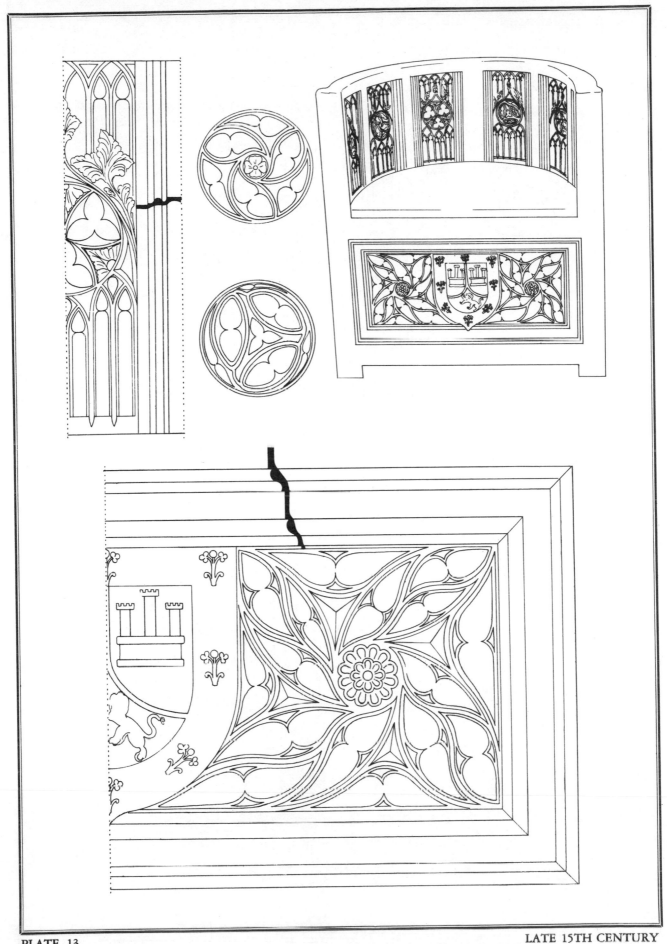

PLATE 13

LATE 15TH CENTURY

"Box" armchair with semicircular base and coat of arms of the Enríquez family, Castilian admirals.

National Archeological Museum, Madrid

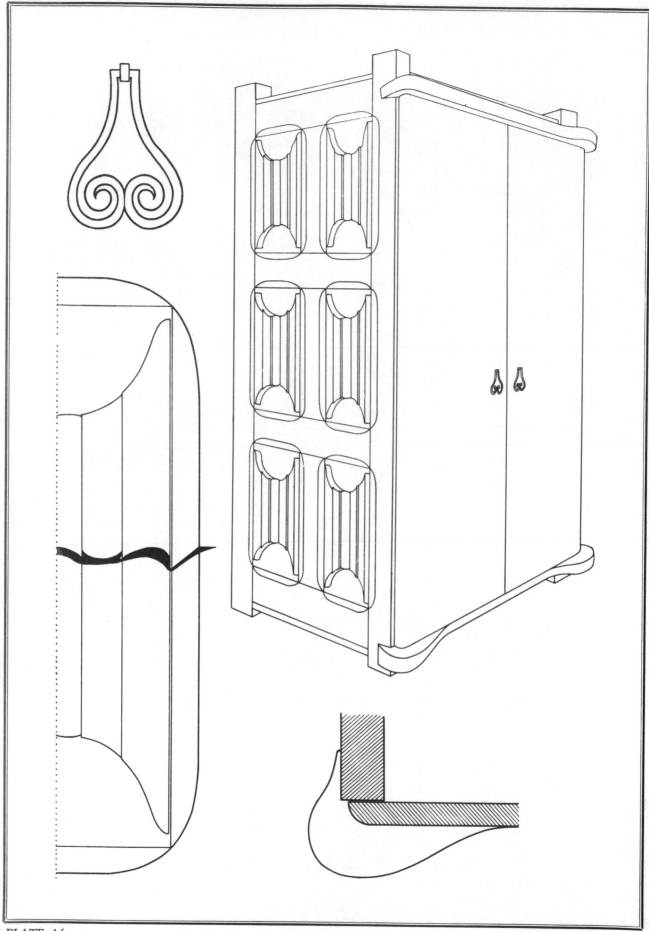

PLATE 14
Gothic wardrobe with "parchment" design.

PLATE 15
Wardrobe with Mudejar decoration of joined wood.

15TH CENTURY

National Archeological Museum, Madrid

PLATE 16
Mudejar writing desk.

15TH CENTURY

Tavera Hospital, Toledo

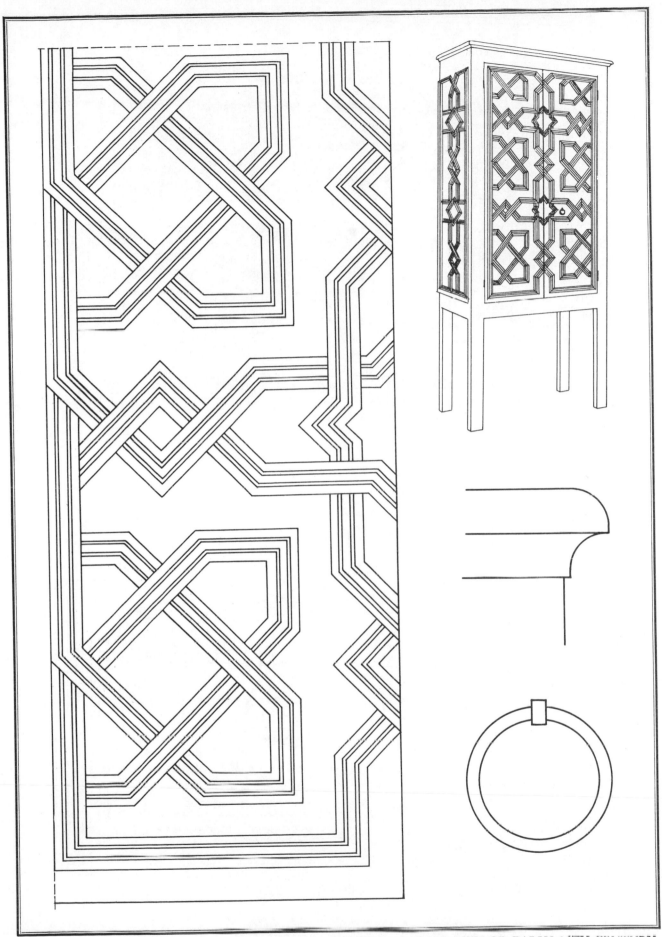

PLATE 17
Mudejar wardrobe.

LATE 15TH OR EARLY 16TH CENTURY

Museum of Art of Catalonia, Barcelona

PLATE 18
Desk decorated with Gothic-Renaissance motifs.

Private collection, Madrid

PLATE 19
Desk of cypress wood decorated with fine Gothic carving.

National Archeological Museum, Madrid

PLATE 20
Mudejar chest with bone inlays.

Lazaro Galdiano Museum, Madrid

PLATE 21
Small chest, with bone inlays, from Granada.

16TH CENTURY

National Archeological Museum, Madrid

PLATE 22
Small Mudejar chest with bone inlays.

16TH CENTURY

26

PLATE 23
Small Mudejar chest with bone inlays.

16TH CENTURY

27

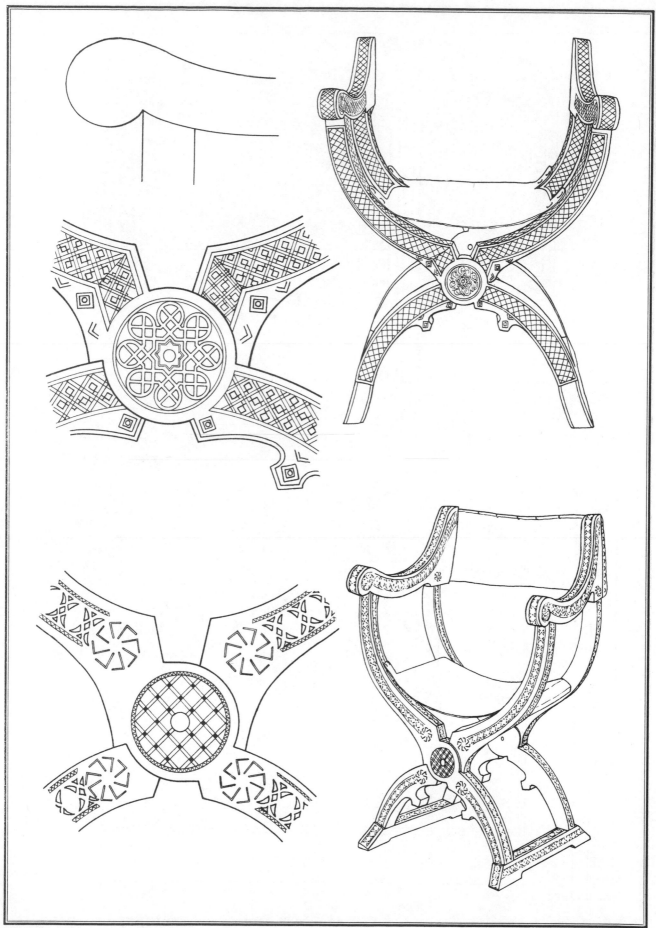

PLATE 24
Mudejar "sidesaddle" or scissors armchairs with bone inlays.

16TH CENTURY

National Archeological Museum, Madrid

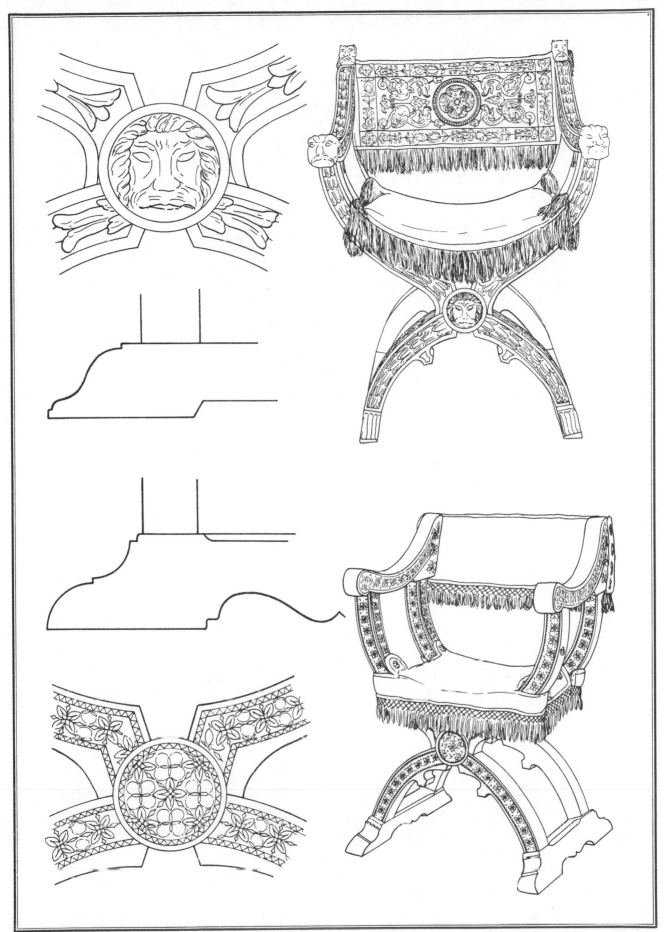

PLATE 25

"Sidesaddle" or scissors armchairs with Renaissance (upper chair) and Mudejar (lower chair) decoration.

Valencia Don Juan Institute, Madrid

PLATE 26
Writing desk with Mudejar marquetry.

National Archeological Museum, Madrid

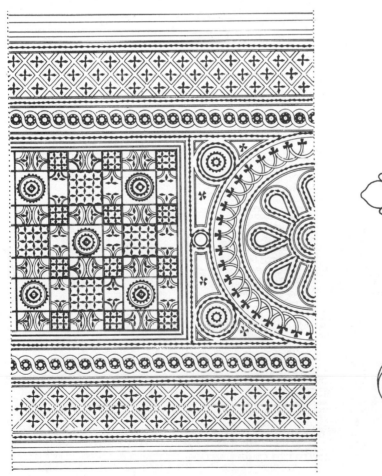

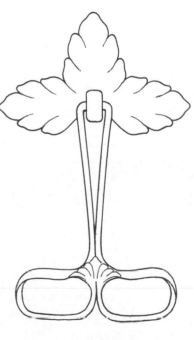

PLATE 27
Desk top with Mudejar marquetry.

16TH CENTURY

National Archeological Museum, Madrid

PLATE 28
Fancy inlaid gilt secretary with Mudejar marquetry.

16TH CENTURY

National Archeological Museum, Madrid

Mudejar marquetry on front of drawers of fancy inlaid gilt secretary.

PLATE 51   16TH CENTURY
Renaissance fancy inlaid gilt secretary with "bridge" base. Mudejar-style marquetry on front of drawers.

Lazaro Galdiano Museum, Madrid

PLATE 32

Seat with Renaissance decoration, reminiscent of Gothic style.

FIRST HALF OF 16TH CENTURY

PLATE 33
Church stall with plateresque carvings.

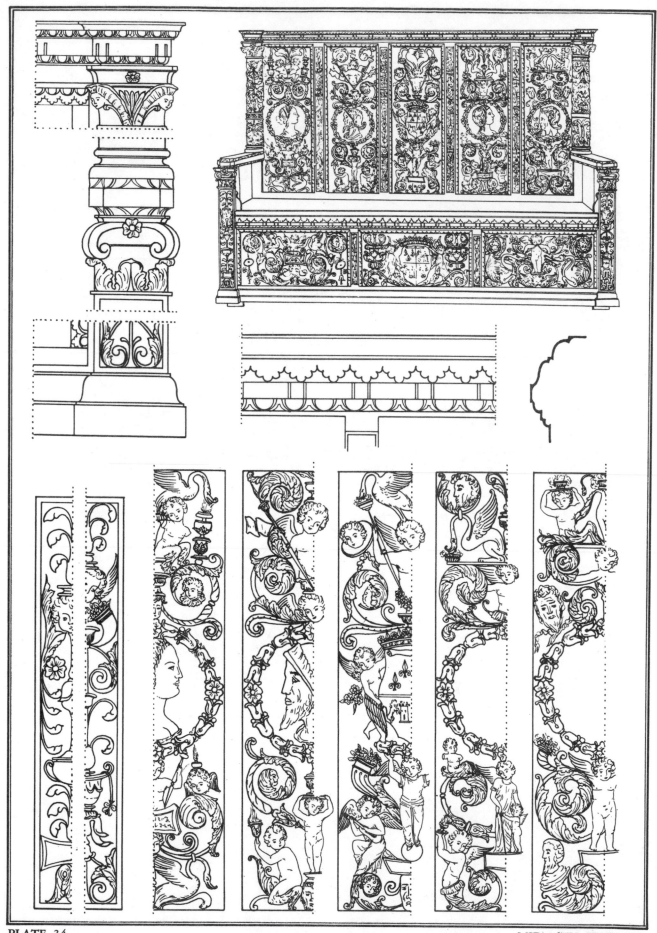

PLATE 34

Oak bench decorated with plateresque carvings with coat of arms of Dukes of Medinaceli.

Collection of Dukes of Medinaceli, Madrid

PLATE 35
Bench decorated with plateresque carvings.

MID 16TH CENTURY

Museum of Decorative Arts, Madrid

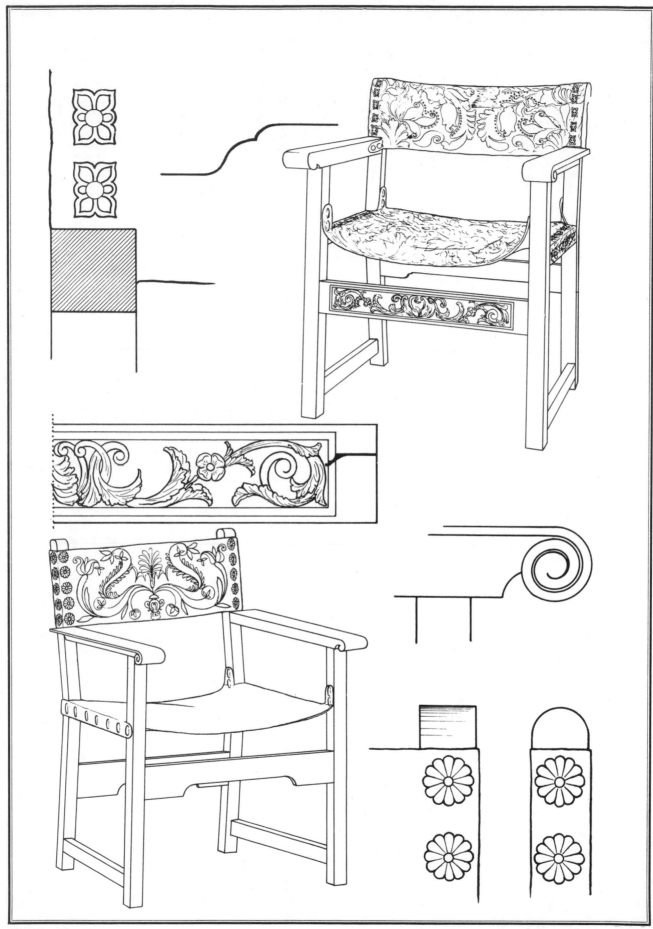

PLATE 36

Friars' armchairs trimmed with multicolored embossed leather.

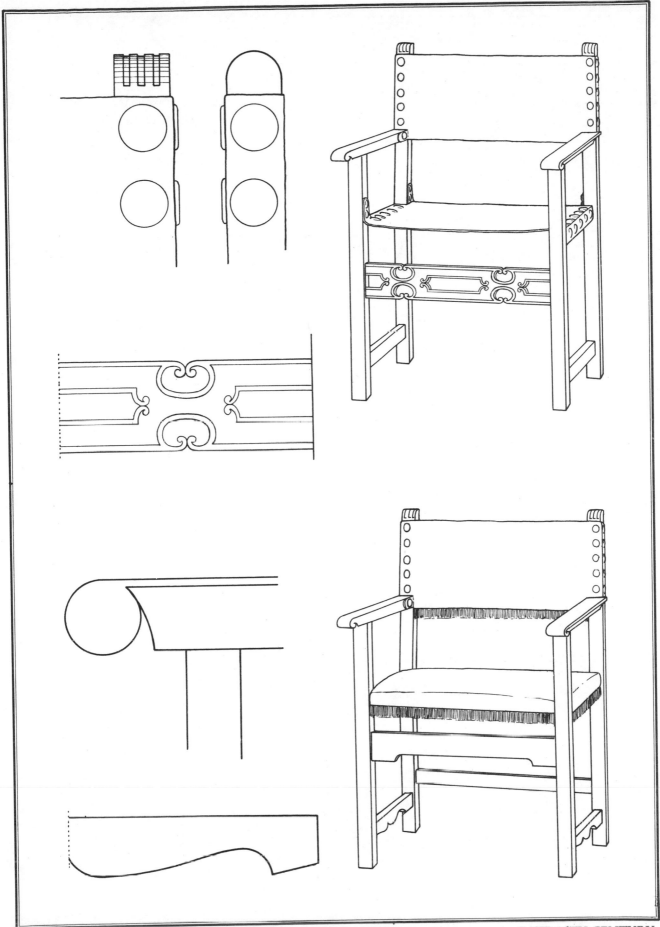

PLATE 37
Friars' armchairs trimmed with leather (upper chair) and cloth (lower chair).

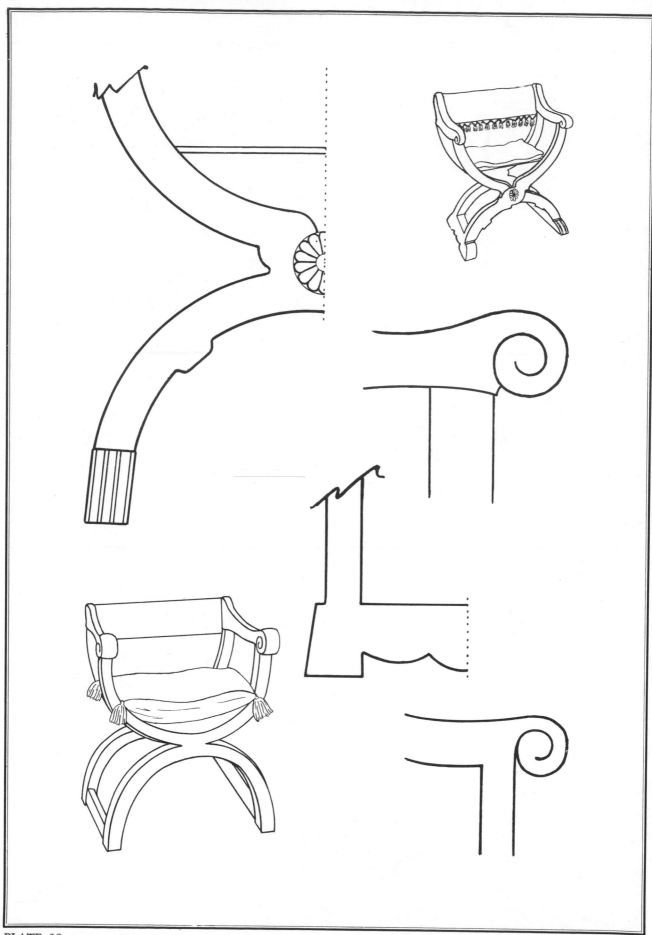

PLATE 38
"Sidesaddle" or scissors chairs.

Casa de las Duenas, Seville

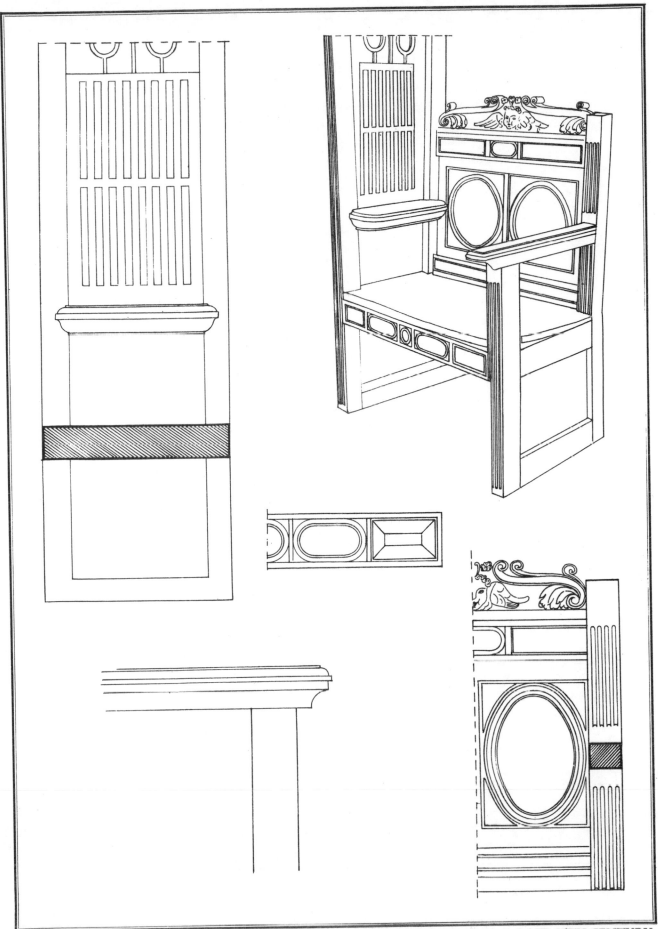

PLATE 39
Armchair-confessional decorated with Renaissance motifs.

Museum of Decorative Arts, Madrid

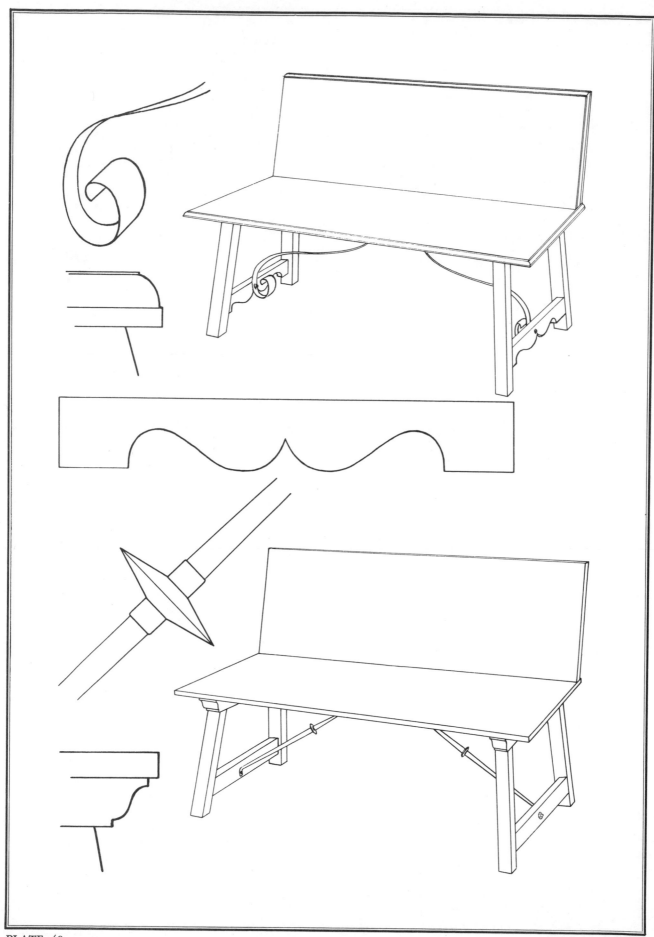

PLATE 40
Benches with wrought-iron ligatures.

Paradors of Merida and Oropesa

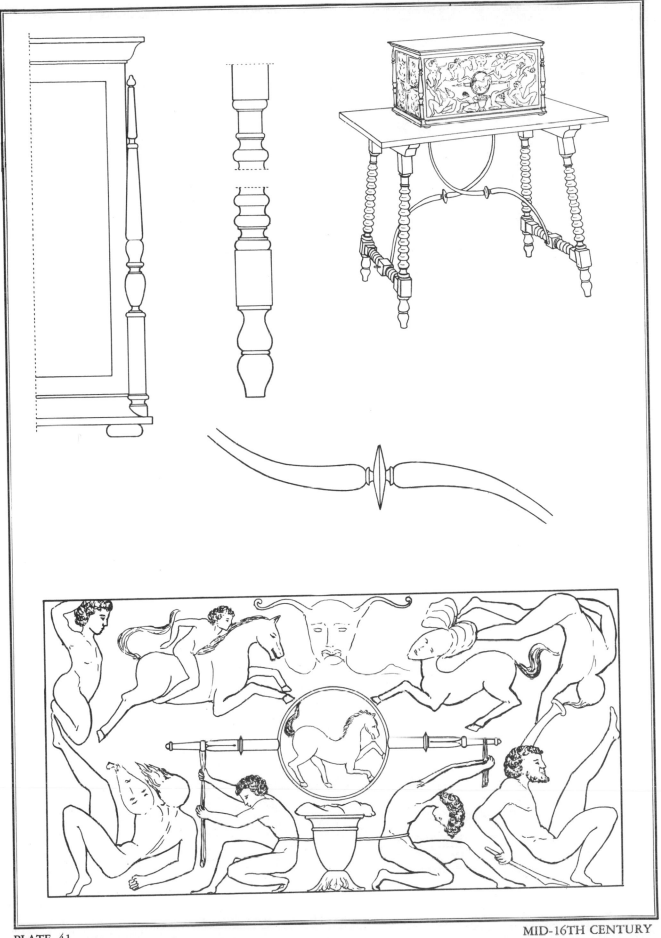

PLATE 41
Chest decorated with Renaissance motifs.

Valencia Don Juan Institute, Madrid

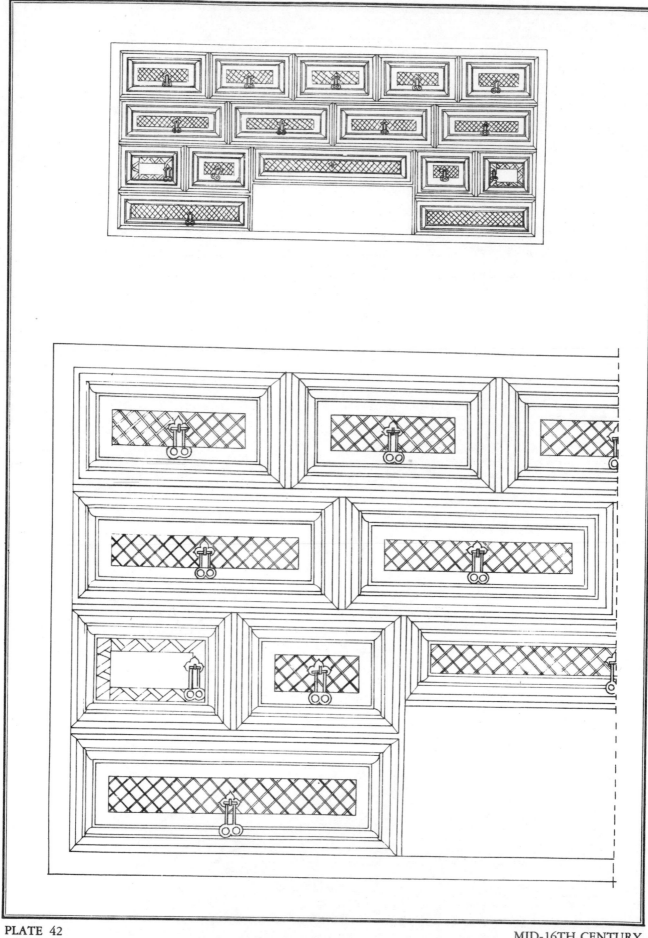

PLATE 42
Fancy inlaid gilt secretary decorated with mouldings and fine Gothic-style carvings.

MID-16TH CENTURY

Museum of Decorative Arts, Madrid

PLATE 43
Desk with "bridge" base and drawers decorated with plateresque carvings.

Private collection

PLATE 44
Desk decorated with Renaissance marquetry, on "bridge" base.

SECOND HALF OF 16TH CENTURY

Museum of Art of Catalonia, Barcelona

PLATE 45
Fancy inlaid gilt secretary with Renaissance marquetry on "bridge" base.

Lazaro Galdiano Museum, Madrid

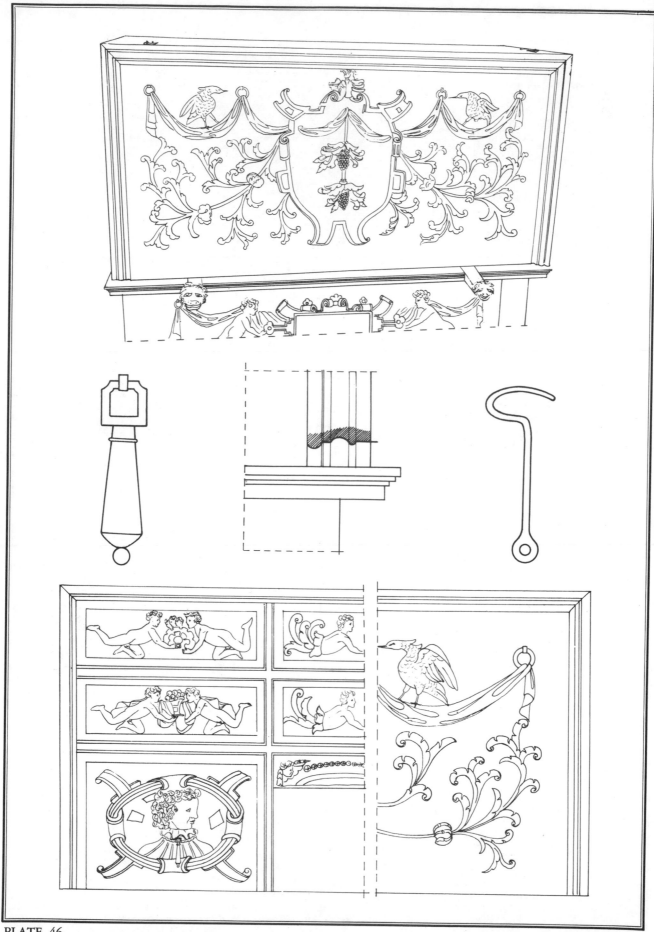

PLATE 46
Desk decorated with Renaissance motifs.

National Archeological Museum, Madrid

PLATE 47
Desk decorated with Renaissance marquetry.

Museum of Decorative Arts, Madrid

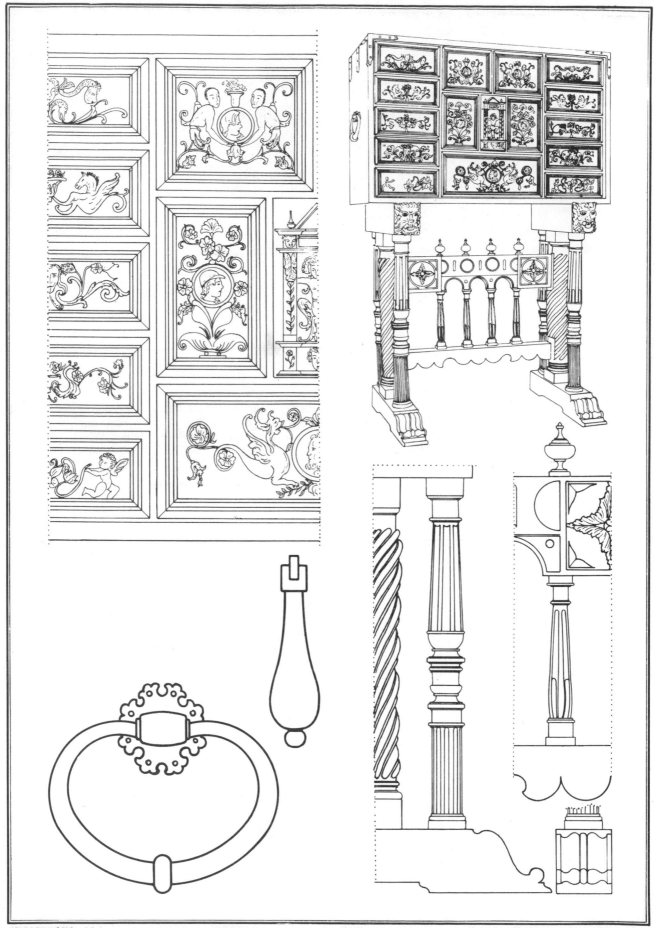

PLATE 48

Fancy inlaid gilt secretary of walnut, decorated with plateresque carvings on a "bridge" base.

PLATE 49
Fancy inlaid gilt secretary decorated with Renaissance carvings.

Museum of Decorative Arts, Madrid

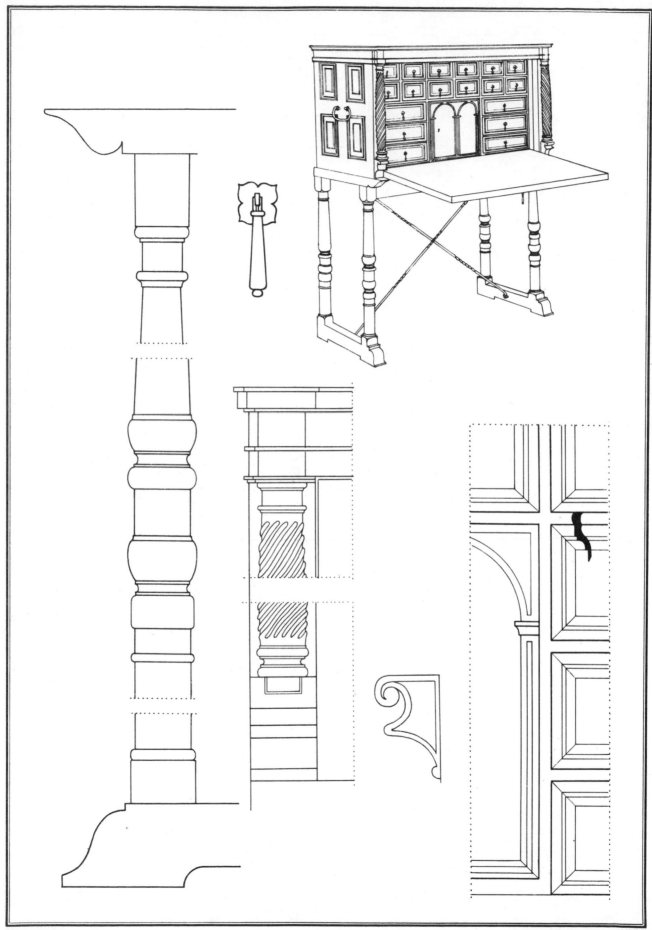

PLATE 50
Desk with Renaissance architectonic motifs.

LATE 16TH CENTURY

Tavera Hospital, Toledo

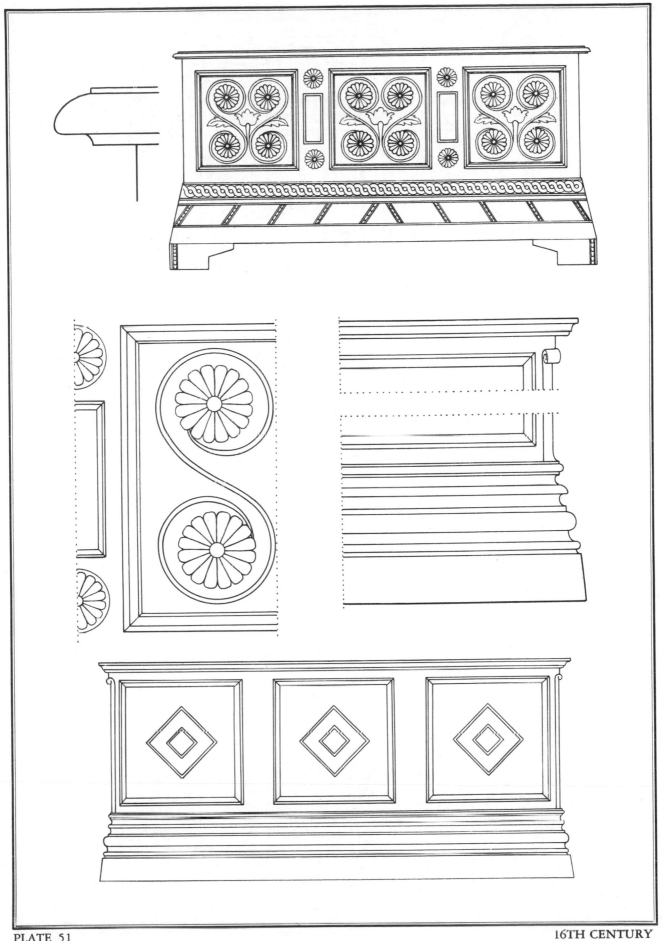

PLATE 51

Large chests decorated with floral and geometric motifs.

Upper chest: Riudabell Castle

PLATE 52
Wardrobe decorated with plateresque carvings.

MID-16TH CENTURY

Paredes de Nava Parochial Church, Palencia

PLATE 53
Wardrobe decorated with plateresque carvings.

National Archeological Museum, Madrid

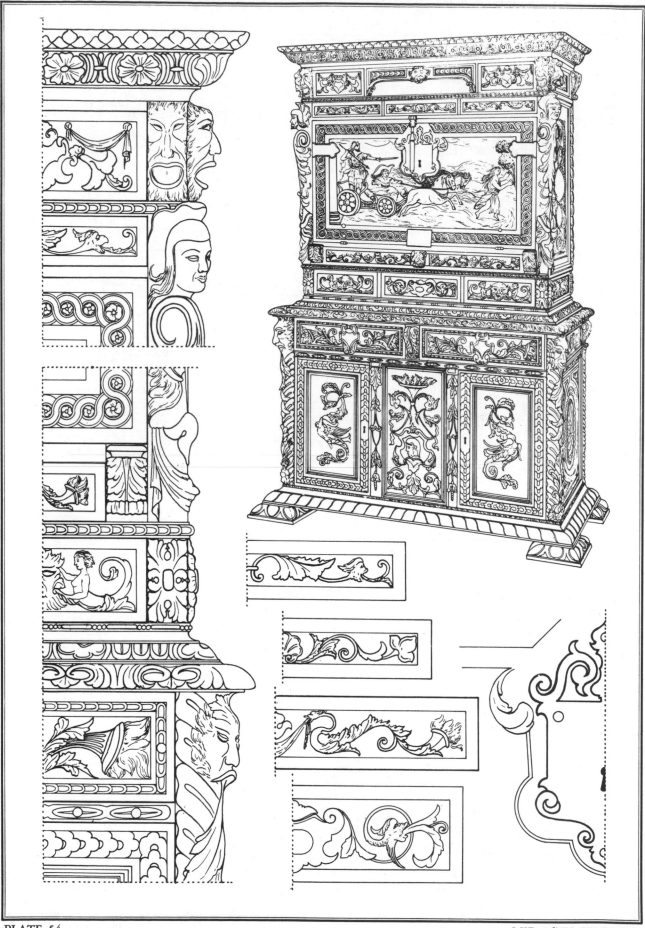

PLATE 54
Chest-on-chest decorated with Renaissance carvings.

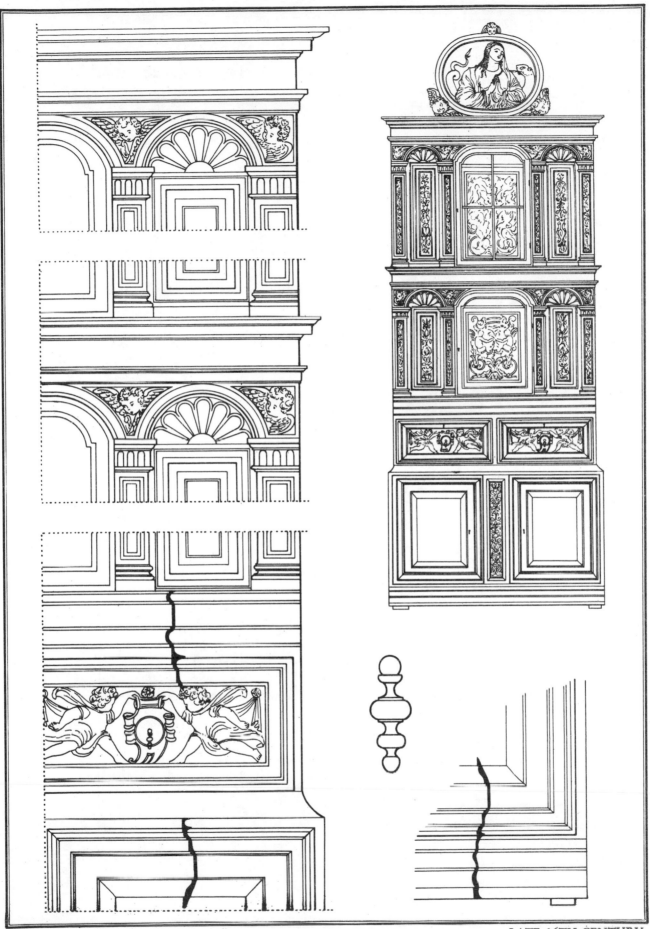

PLATE 55
Wardrobe decorated with Renaissance carvings.

Private collection

PLATE 56

MID-16TH CENTURY

Chest-on-chest decorated with Renaissance carvings.

PLATE 57

Chest-on-chest decorated with Renaissance carvings and Gothic-style "parchments."

PLATE 58
Chest-on-chest decorated with Renaissance carvings and Gothic-style "parchments."

MID-16TH CENTURY

PLATE 59
Desk decorated with Renaissance carvings.

MID-16TH CENTURY

PLATE 60
Italian-style desk decorated with Renaissance carvings.

PLATE 61
Italian-style desk decorated with Renaissance carvings.

PLATE 62
Italian-style chest-on-chest decorated with Renaissance carvings.

MID-16TH CENTURY

Museum of Art of Catalonia, Barcelona

PLATE 63
Large wardrobe-chest decorated with plateresque carvings.

MID-16TH CENTURY

Chapel of the Constable, Cathedral of Burgos

PLATE 64
Writing desks with pyramidal construction and ligatures of wrought iron.

PLATE 65
Chest-on-chest decorated with Renaissance carvings.

SECOND HALF OF 16TH CENTURY

Lazaro Galdiano Museum, Madrid

PLATE 66
Heads of wrought-iron nails.

16TH CENTURY

Lazaro Galdiano Museum, Madrid

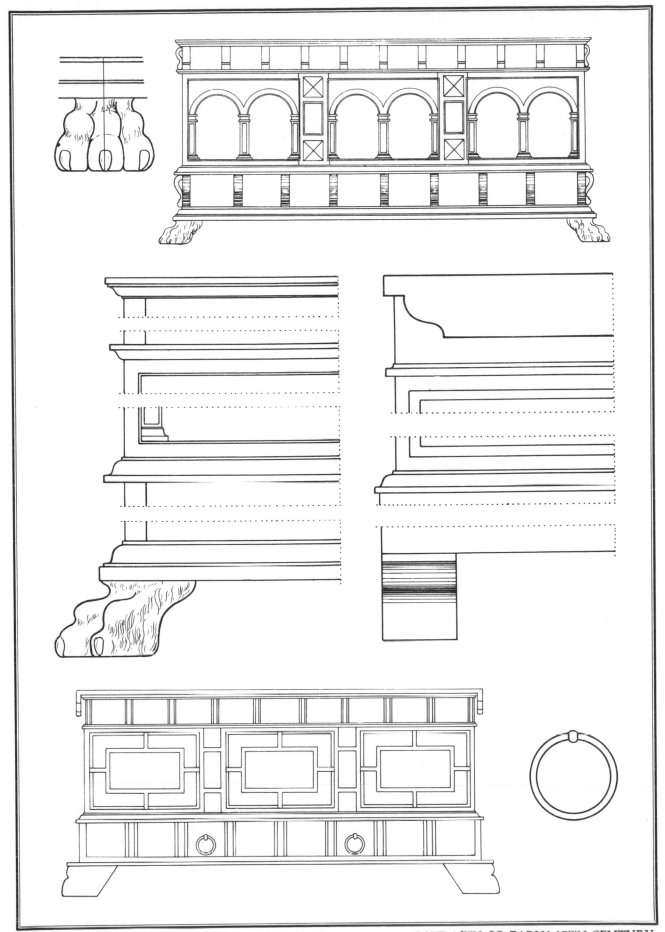

PLATE 67
Large chests of Renaissance design.

Riudabell Castle

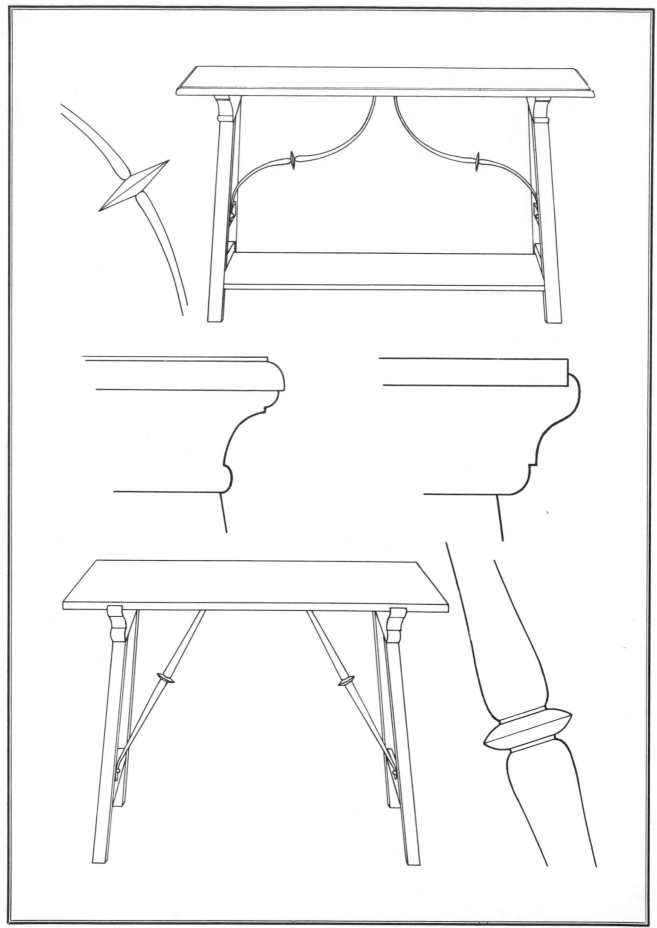

PLATE 68   LATE 16TH OR EARLY 17TH CENTURY
Writing desks with pyramidal construction and ligatures of wrought iron.

Museum of Bilbao and Parador of Santillano, Santander

PLATE 69
Carved panels with plateresque motifs.

From the doors of the Alcazar of Toledo, which were destroyed in 1936

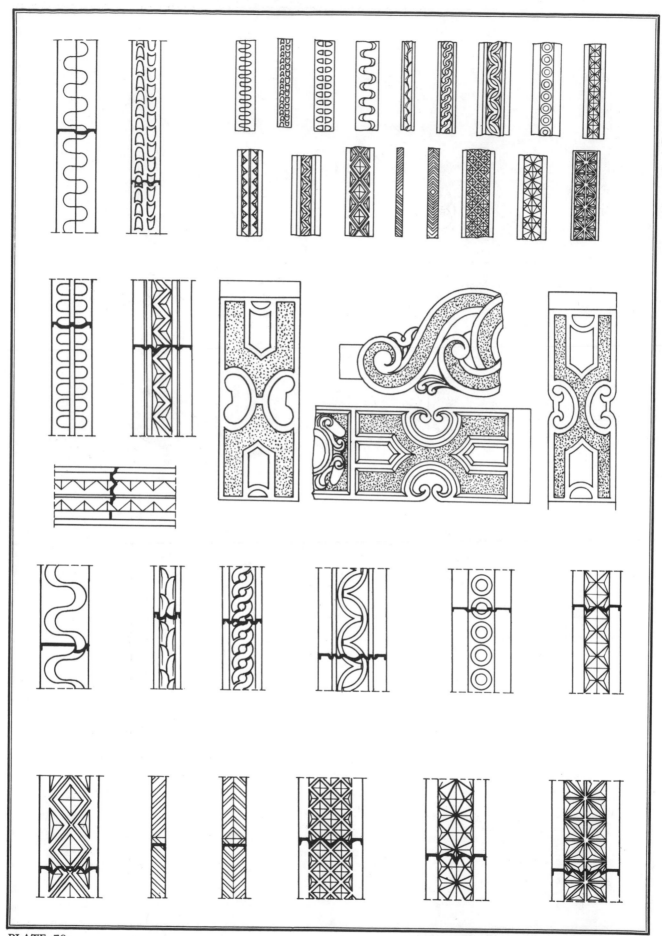

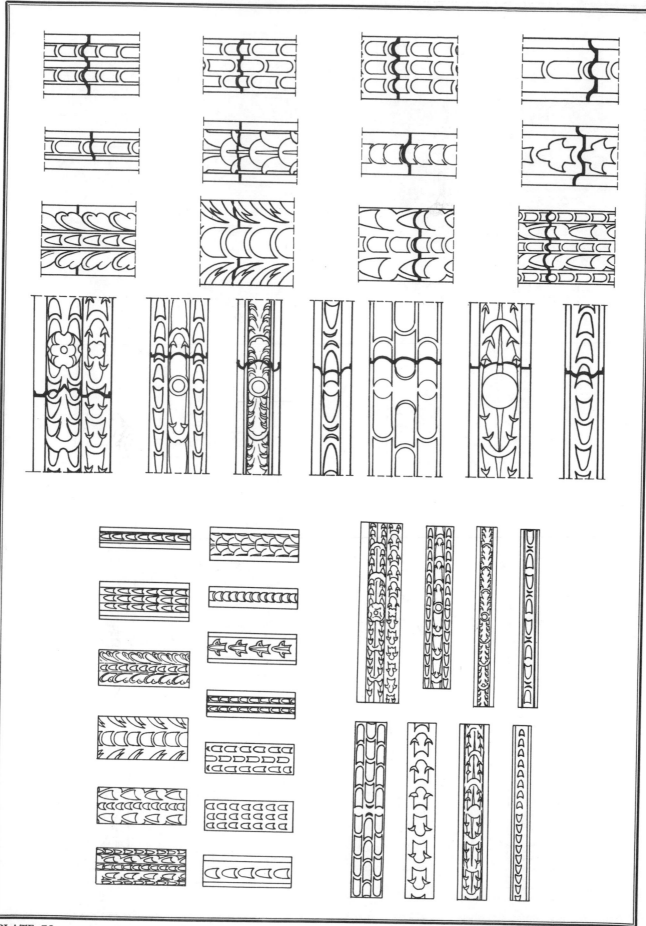

PLATE 73
Leather chest decorated with metal nails and gilt ironwork.

17TH CENTURY

Museum of Decorative Arts, Madrid

77

PLATE 74
Small chest decorated with gilt ironwork.

National Archeological Museum, Madrid

PLATE 75
Small wooden chest with carved decoration.

Museum of Decorative Arts, Madrid

PLATE 76
Wooden chest decorated with baroque carvings.

17TH CENTURY

March collection, Palma de Mallorca

PLATE 77
Wardrobes with panelled doors.

Gustavo Gili Collection, Santillana del Mar

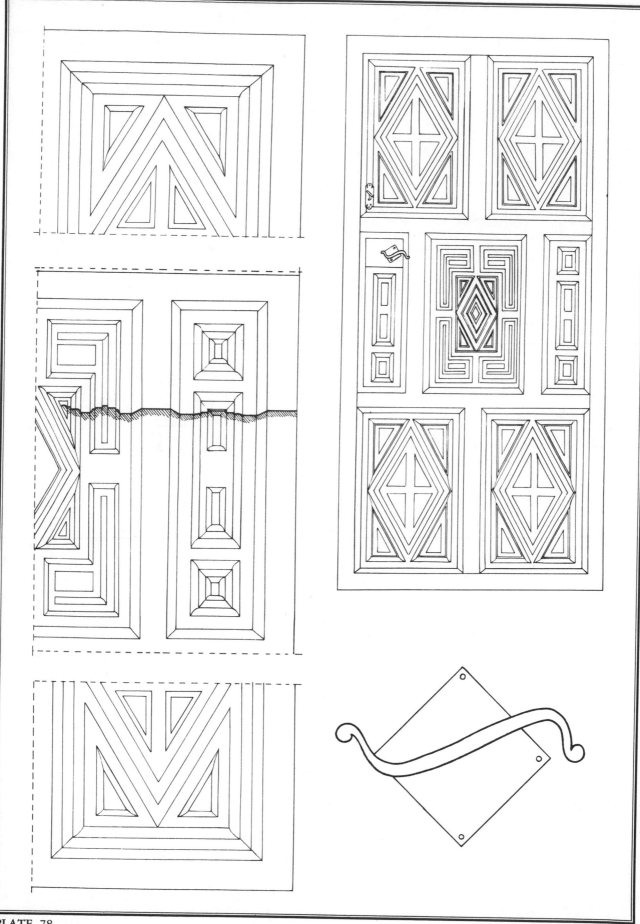

PLATE 78
Door decorated with geometric motifs.

17TH CENTURY

Arciprestal de Santa Maria, Castellon

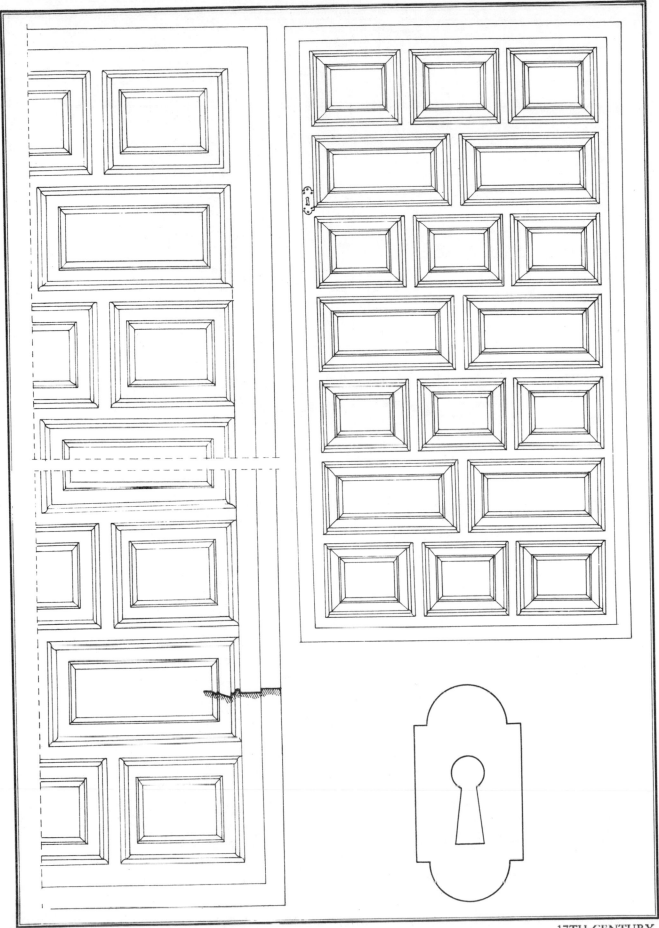

PLATE 79
Panelled door.

Private collection

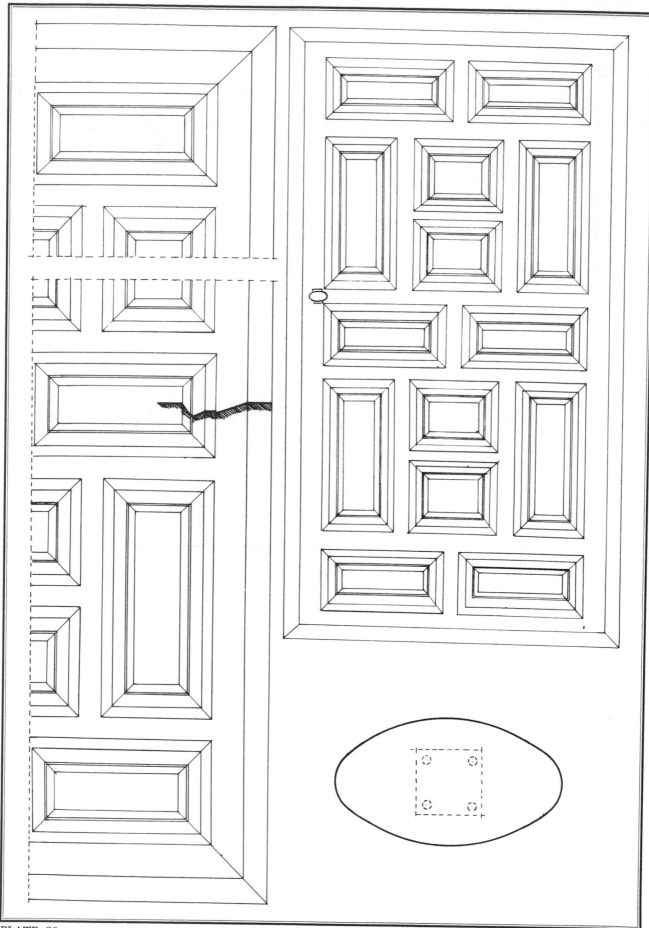

PLATE 80
Panelled door.

Private collection

PLATE 81
Wardrobe decorated with carvings and turned balusters.

Museum of Decorative Arts, Madrid

PLATE 82
Wardrobe decorated with zigzag moulding.

Tavera Hospital, Toledo

PLATE 83
Wardrobe with turned balusters on doors.

Museum of Decorative Arts, Madrid

PLATE 84
Low wardrobe decorated with mouldings.

17TH CENTURY

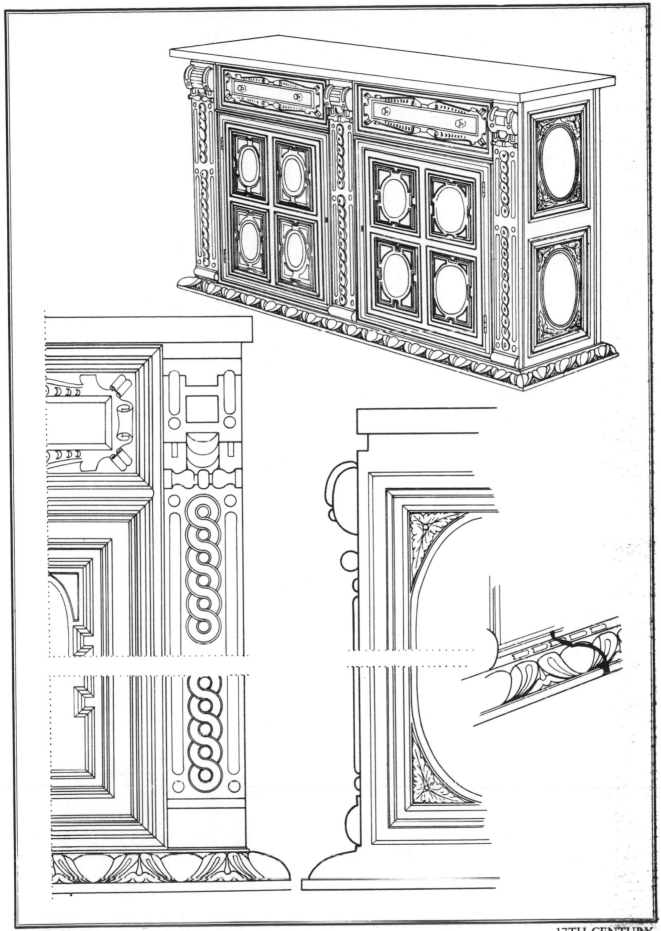

PLATE 85
Low wardrobe decorated with baroque carvings.

PLATE 86
Low wardrobe decorated with baroque carvings and twisted columns.

Museum of Painting, Seville

PLATE 87
Wardrobe with latticework and turned balusters.

Private collection

PLATE 88

Low wardrobe decorated with mouldings and baroque carvings.

PLATE 89
Wardrobe completely decorated with baroque carvings.

PLATE 90
Low wardrobe with decoration showing Central European influence.

PLATE 91
Chest-on-chest decorated with baroque carvings and turned balusters.

Private collection

PLATE 92
Chest-on-chest decorated with baroque carvings and turned balusters.

Private collection

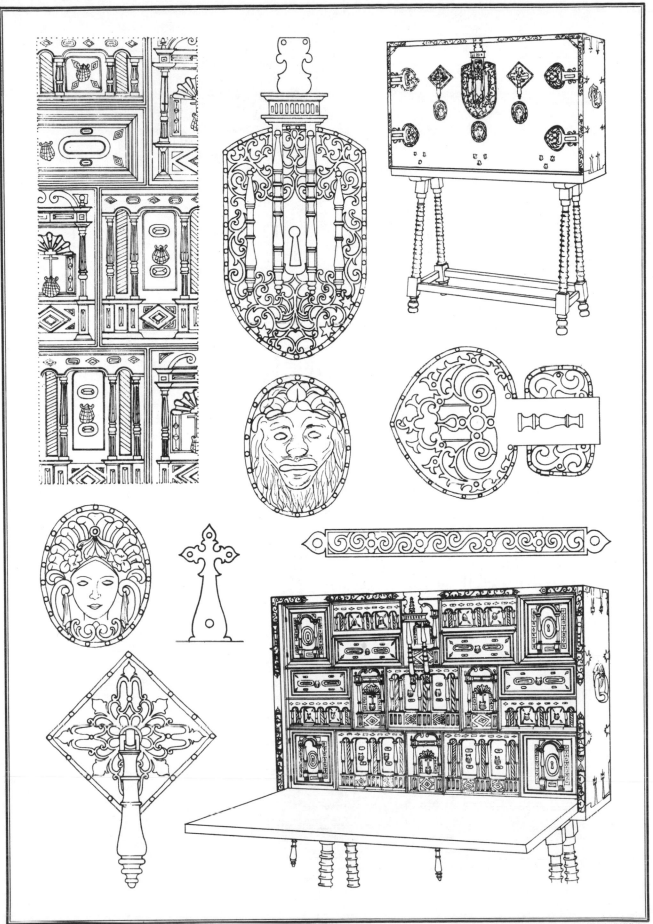

PLATE 93   FIRST HALF OF 17TH CENTURY
Desk decorated with pieces of multicolored and gilt bone. Top with fine gilt ironwork. Writing table with turned legs.
Tavera Hospital, Toledo

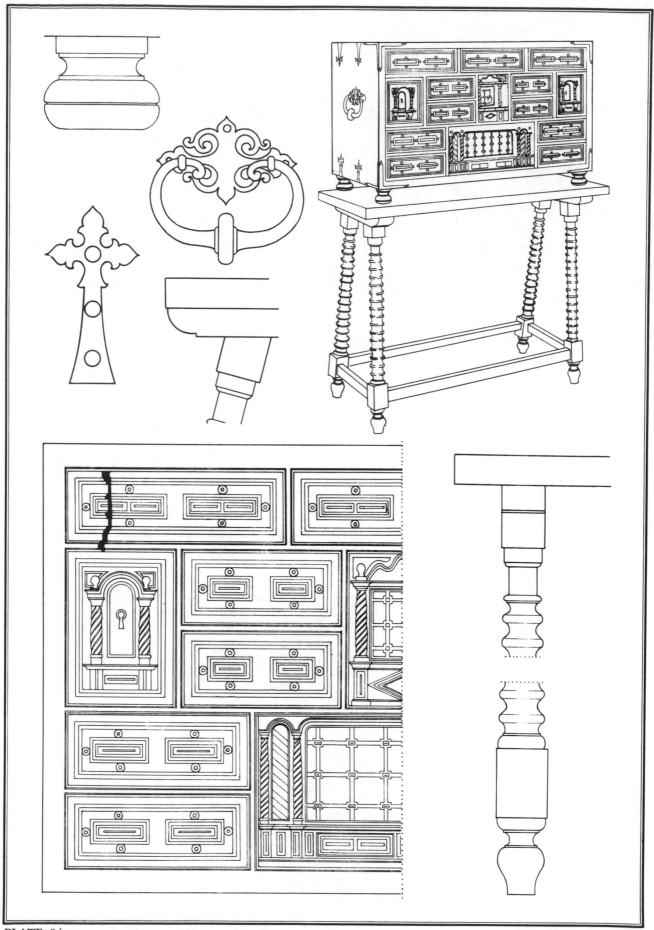

PLATE 94
Fancy inlaid gilt secretary decorated with mouldings and small turned posts.

MID-17TH CENTURY

Tavera Hospital, Toledo

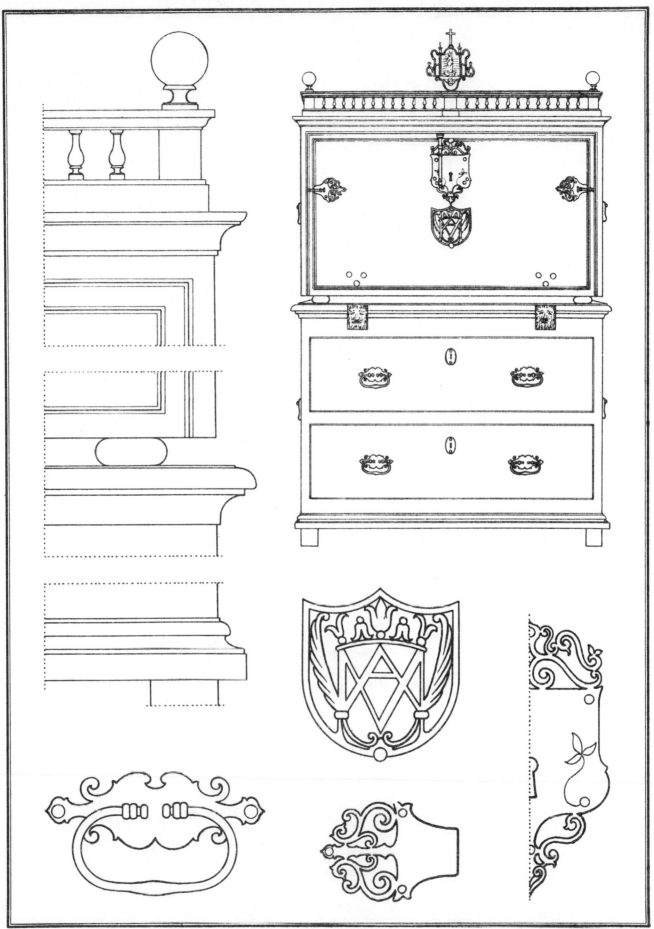

PLATE 95
Desk on top of chest of drawers with gilt hardware.

FIRST HALF OF 17TH CENTURY

Cervantes' house, Valladolid

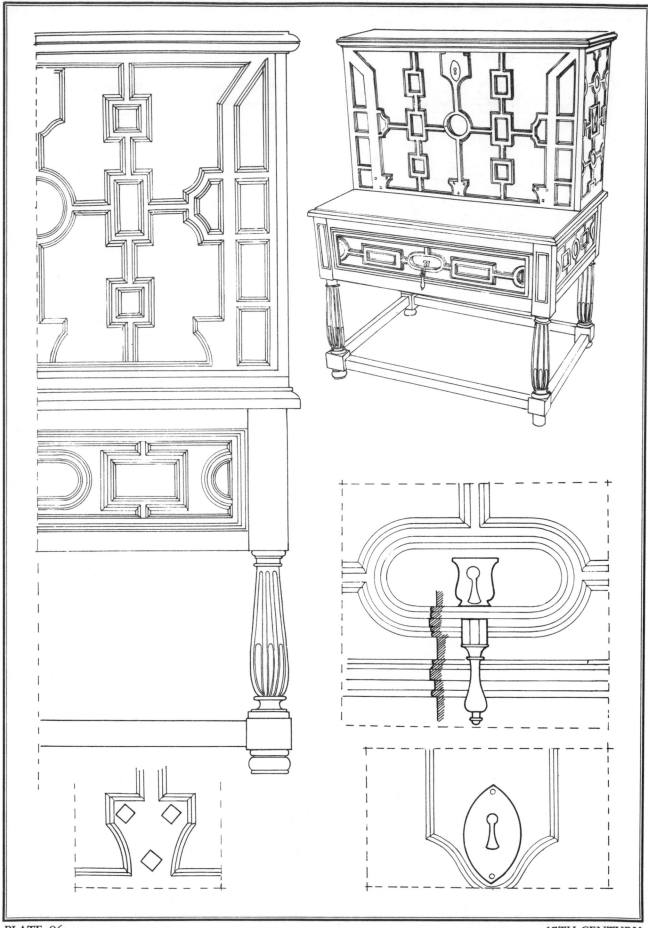

PLATE 96
Desk decorated with mouldings.

17TH CENTURY

National Archeological Museum, Madrid

PLATE 97
Fancy gilt secretary decorated with inlaid bone.

MID-17TH CENTURY

National Archeological Museum, Madrid

PLATE 98
Fancy inlaid gilt secretary decorated with bone plaques with ornamental engraving.

Lazaro Galdiano Museum, Madrid

PLATE 99
Small wooden chest decorated with burned engravings.

MID-17TH CENTURY

Tavera Hospital, Toledo

PLATE 100
Small desk decorated with bone marquetry.

MID-17TH CENTURY

Tavera Hospital, Toledo

PLATE 101   MID-17TH CENTURY

Fancy inlaid gilt secretary decorated with engraved plaques of bone, on pedestal in form of inverted truncated rectangular pyramids.

PLATE 102
Desk on base of twisted columns.

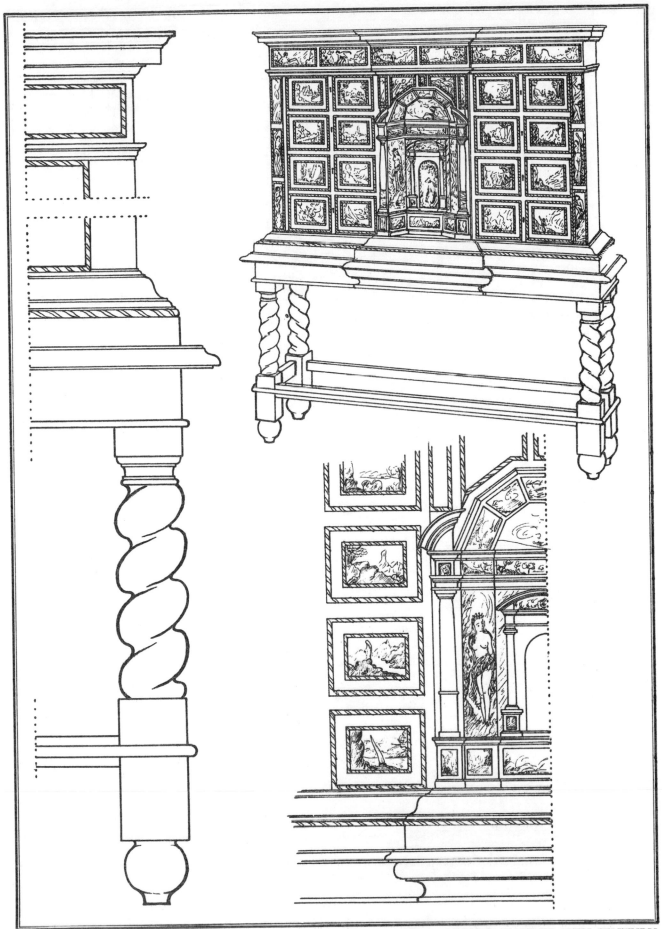

PLATE 103
Fancy inlaid gilt secretary decorated with painted mirrors, on a base of twisted columns.

PLATE 104

Fancy inlaid gilt secretary decorated with tortoiseshell plaques and gilt metal locks and decorative lines.

Private collection

PLATE 105

SECOND HALF OF 17TH CENTURY

Fancy inlaid gilt secretary covered with tortoiseshell, with openwork cornice and gilt metal lines and decorations.

Private collection

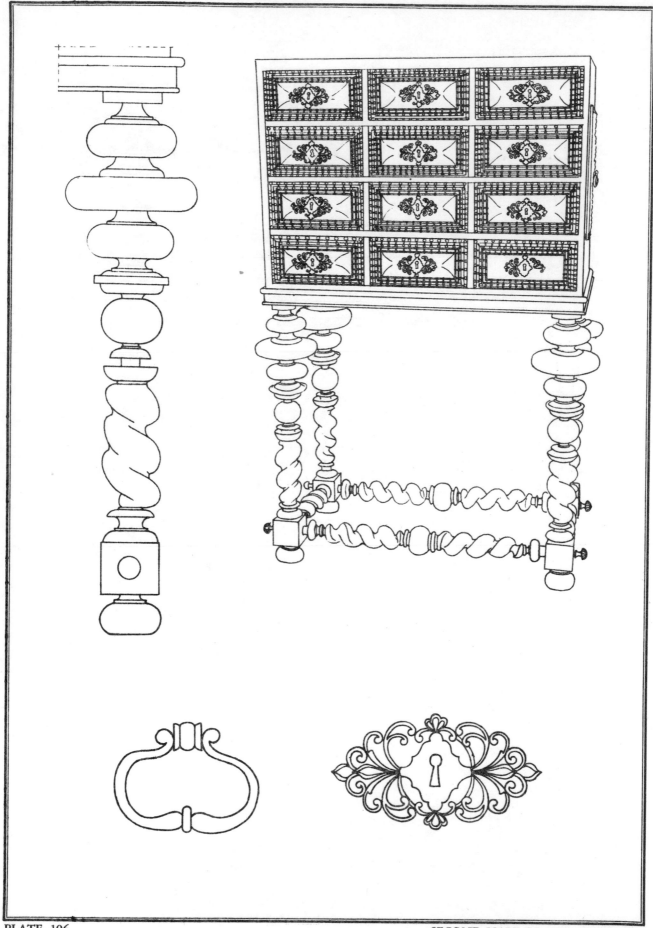

PLATE 106   SECOND HALF OF 17TH CENTURY

Portuguese-style counter. Drawers decorated with rippled ebony mouldings. Base of twisted columns.

Museum of Decorative Arts, Madrid

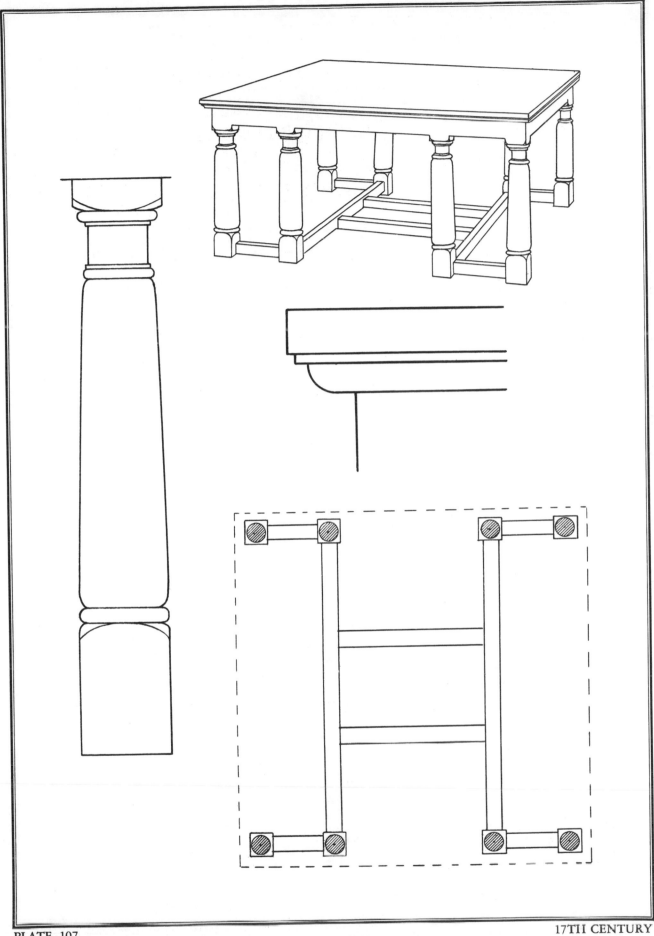

PLATE 107
Table with eight legs joined by wooden beams.

Riudabell Castle

PLATE 108
Folding table with turned legs.

Gustavo Gili collection, Santillana del Mar

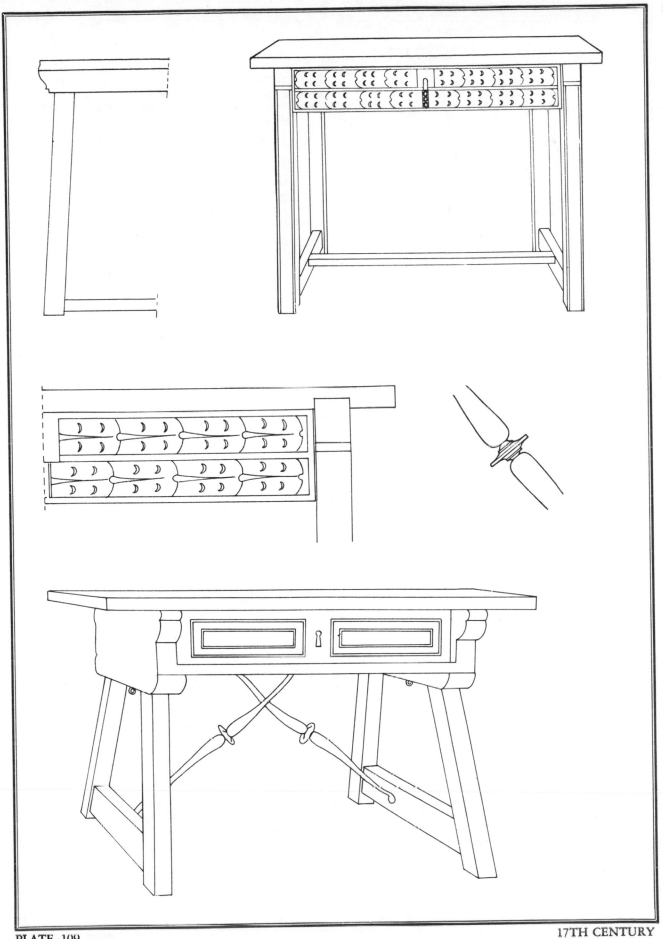

PLATE 110
Table with carved drawer fronts and a "bridge" base.

Museum of Decorative Arts, Madrid

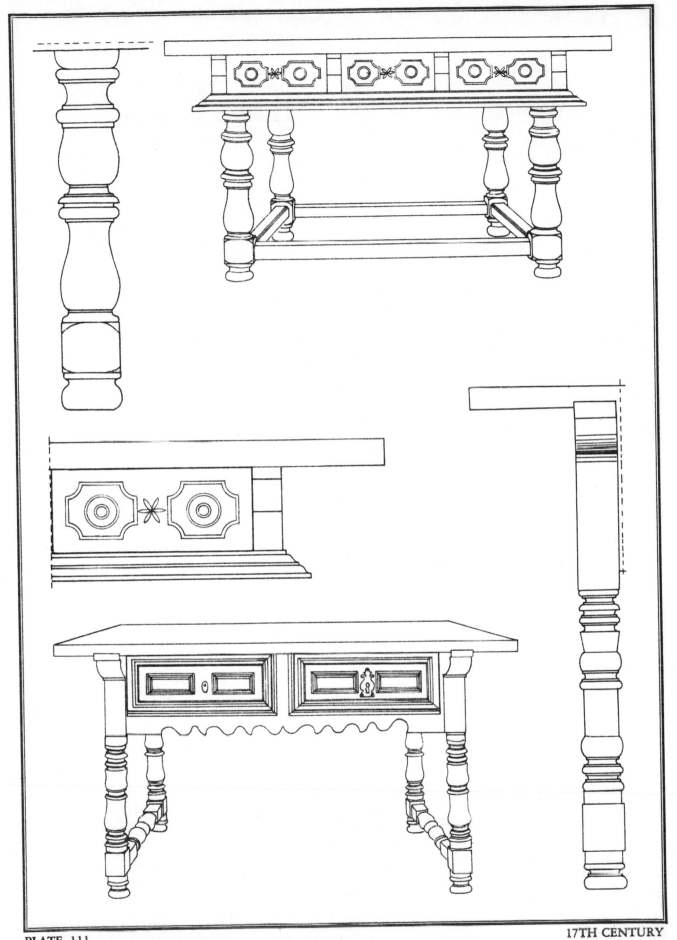

PLATE 111
Tables with turned legs and drawers decorated with mouldings.

Municipal Museum, Romantic Museum and Fundaciones Vega Inclán, Madrid

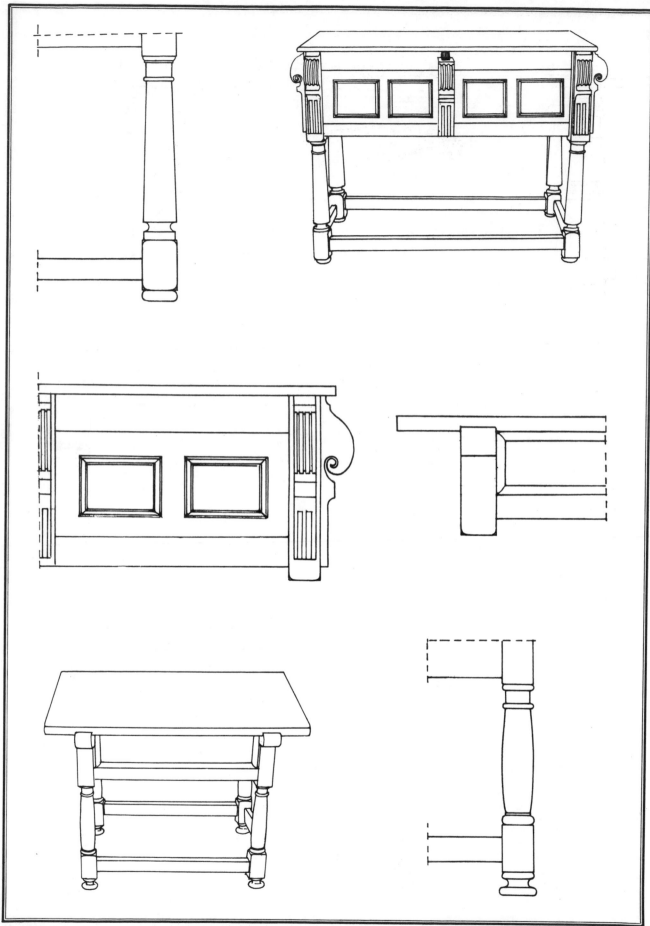

PLATE 112
Portable table.

FIRST HALF OF 17TH CENTURY

Museum of Decorative Arts, Madrid

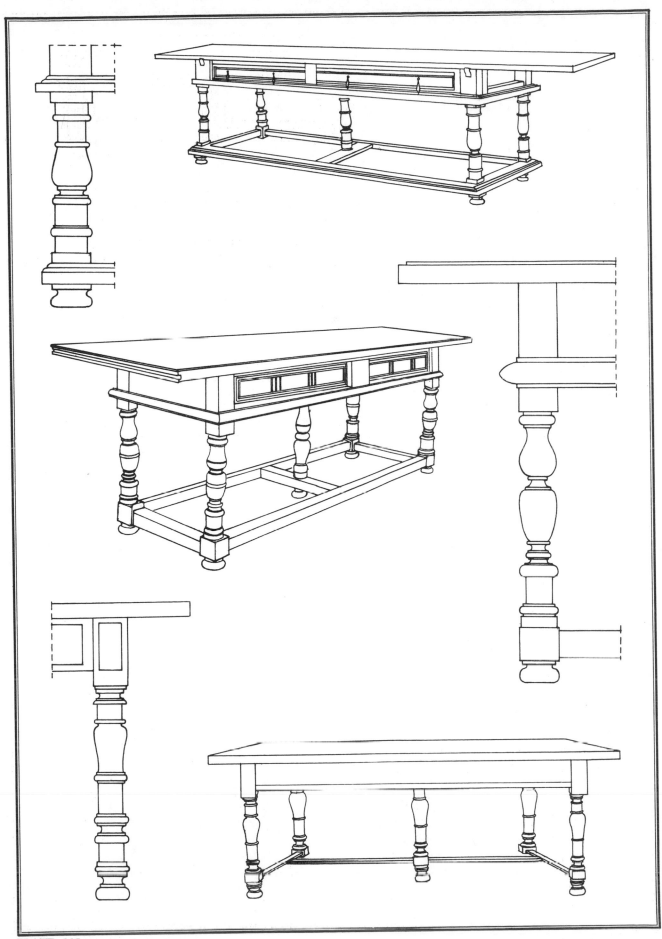

PLATE 113
Table-counter with turned legs.

Museum of Decorative Arts, Madrid

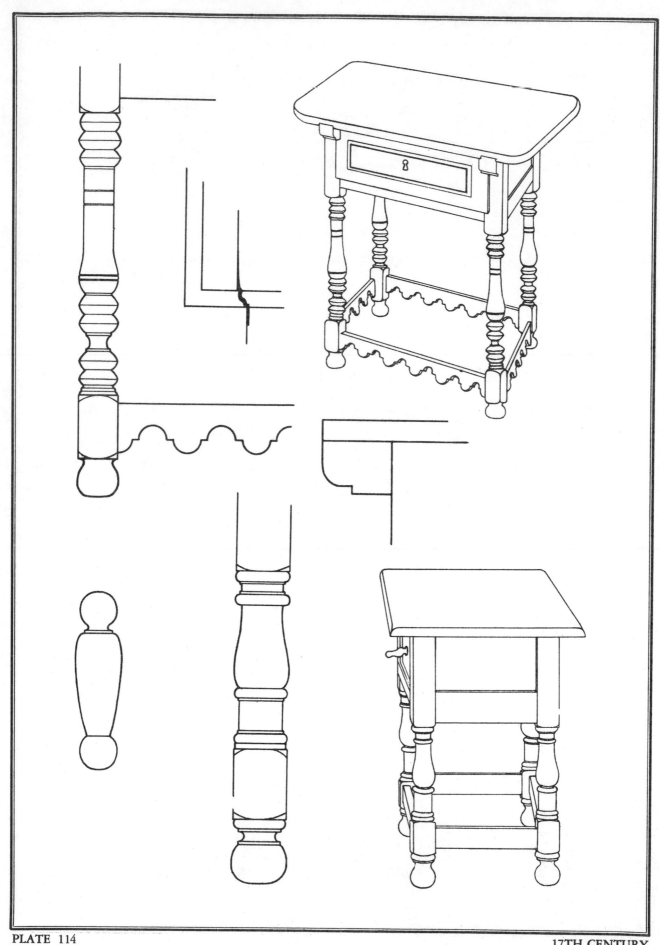

PLATE 114
Small portable tables with turned legs.

Lope de Vega's house, Madrid, and private collection, Granada

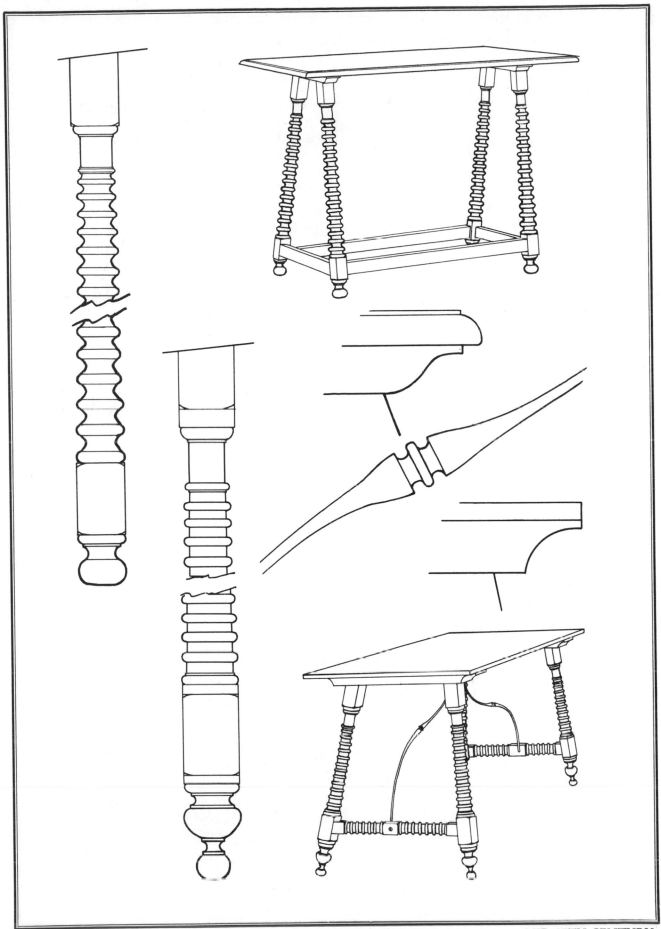

PLATE 115
Pyramid-base writing tables with turned legs.

Museum of Bilbao and Casa Dameto, Palma de Mallorca

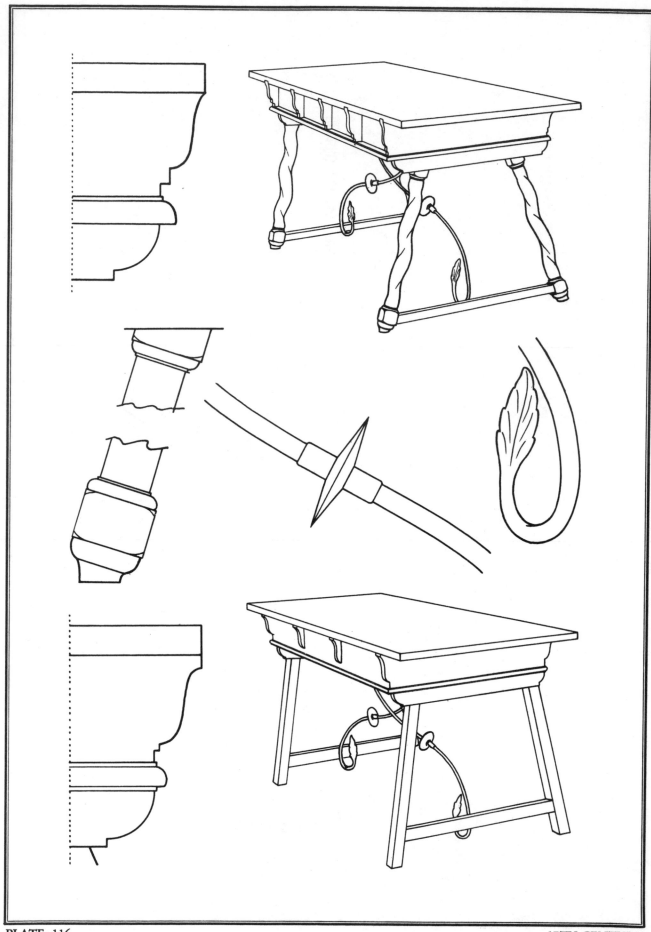

PLATE 116
Pyramid-base writing tables with wrought-iron ligatures.

17TH CENTURY

Parador of Santillana del Mar

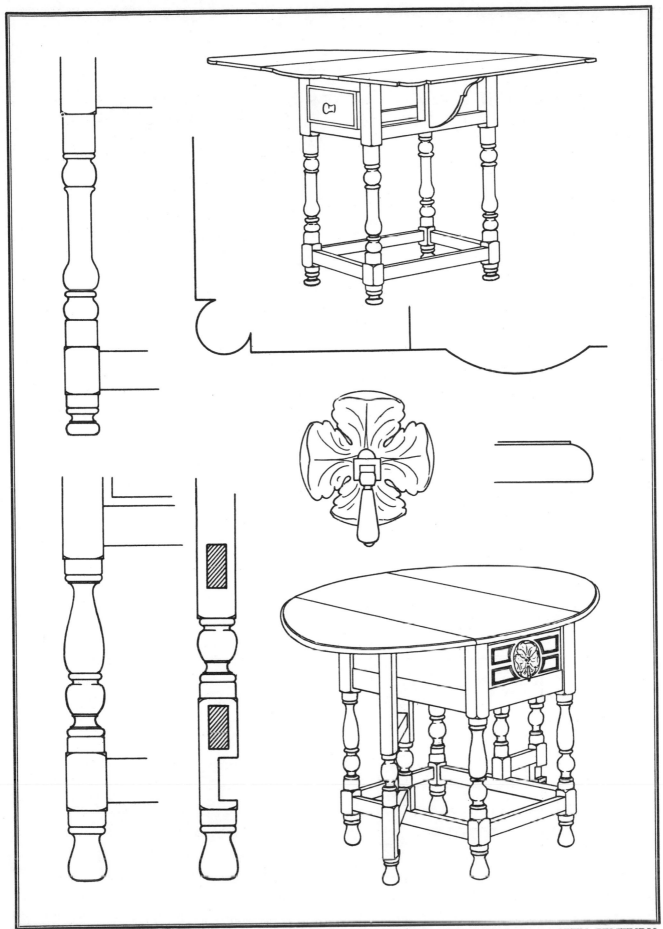

PLATE 117
Folding tables with turned legs.

Parador of Gredos, Avila and Parador of Ubeda, Jaen

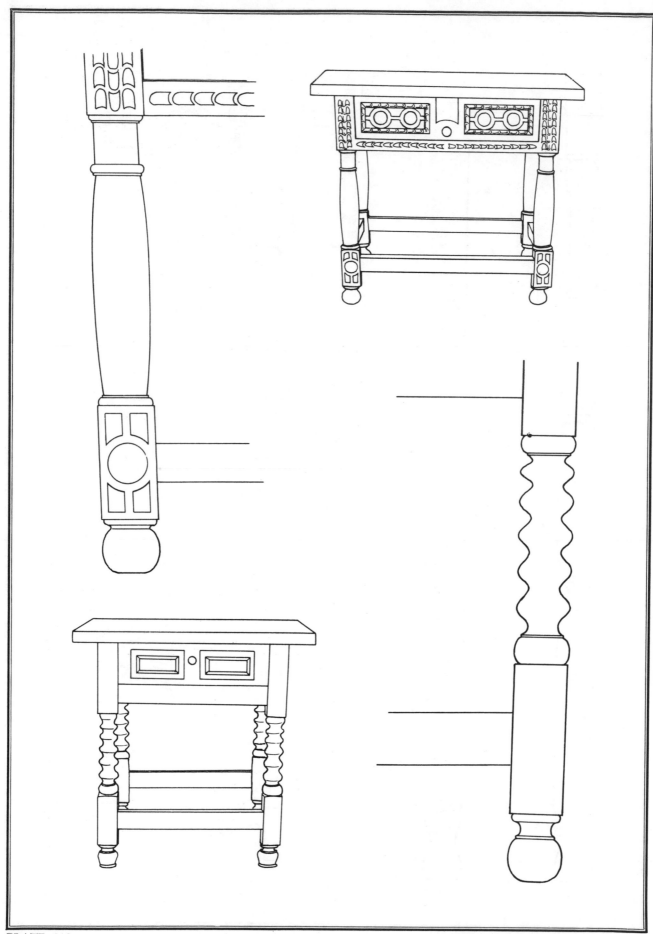

PLATE 118
Small portable table decorated with carved tracery.

FIRST HALF OF 17TH CENTURY

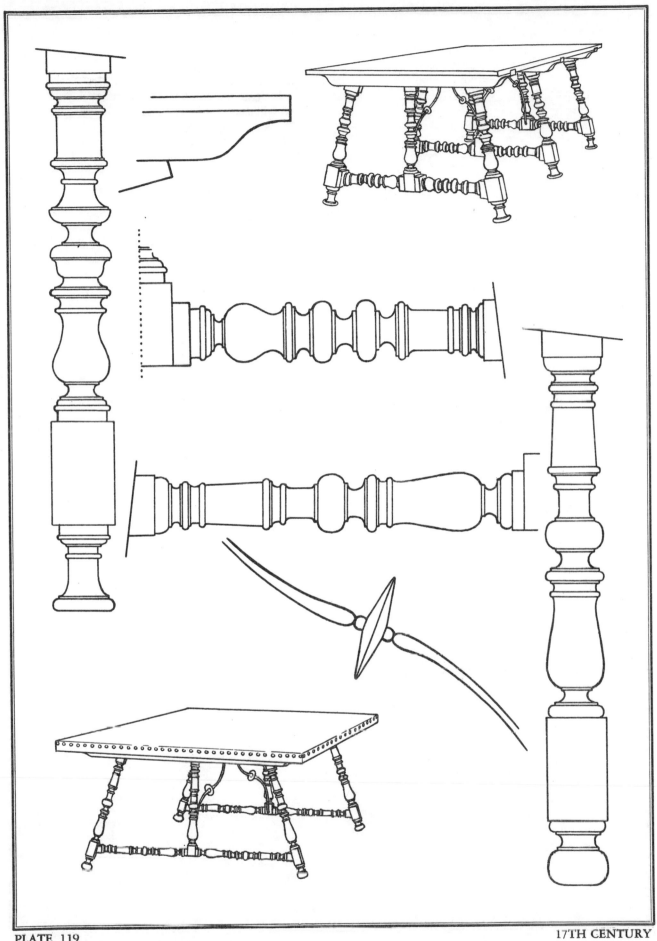

PLATE 119

17TH CENTURY

Small portable tables with turned legs and wrought-iron ligatures.

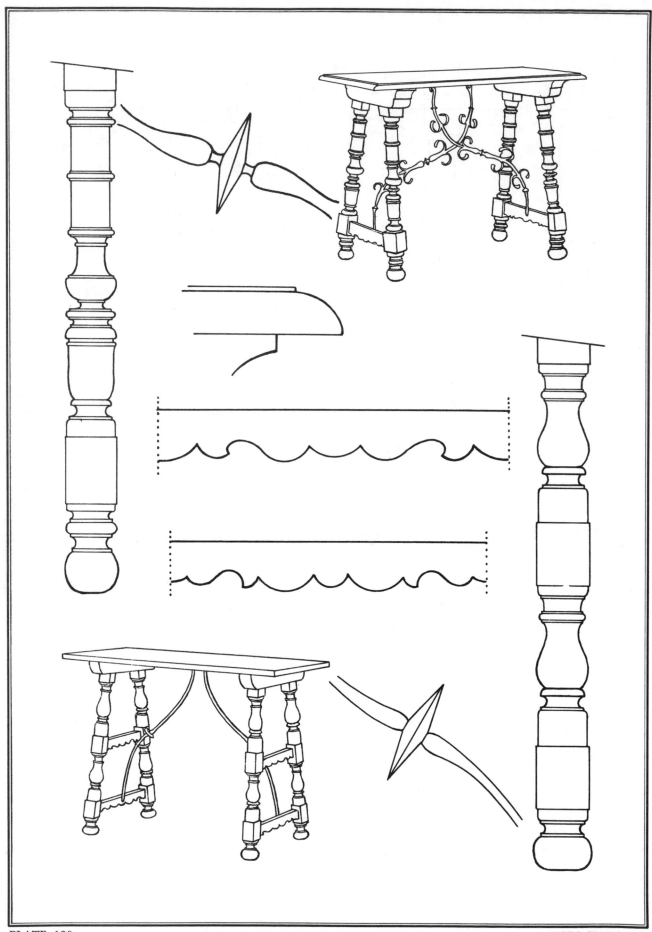

PLATE 120

Small writing tables with turned legs and wrought-iron ligatures.

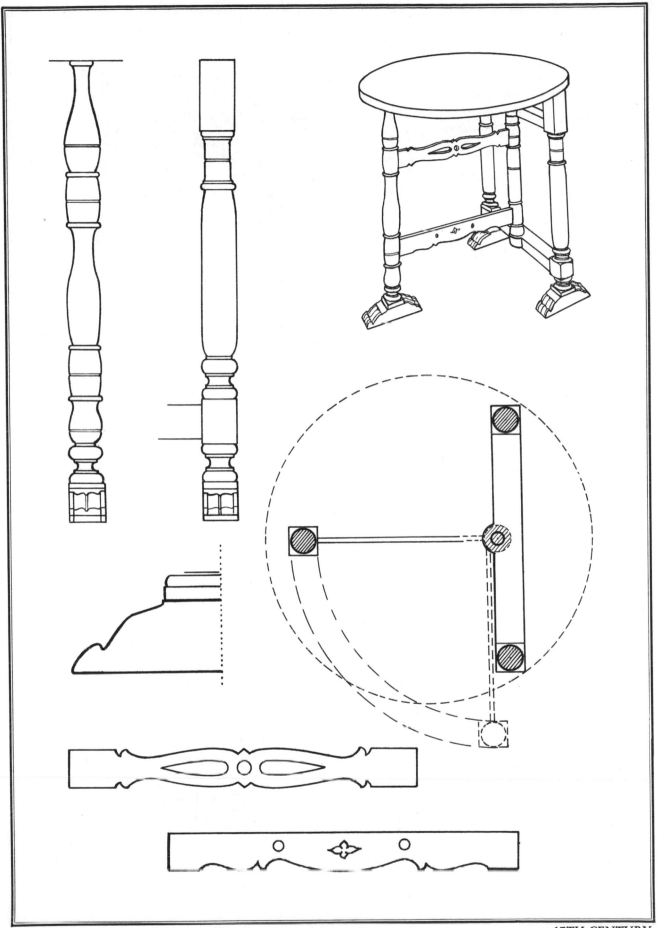

PLATE 121   17TH CENTURY
Small folding table with a round top and turned legs.

PLATE 122
Table decorated with carvings of folk art.

PLATE 123

Table with turned wooden legs and crosspieces; drawer fronts decorated with folk art carvings.

PLATE 124
Tables with legs decorated with wavy or spiral stria.

PLATE 125

17TH CENTURY

Table with turned legs and carved decoration on the front.

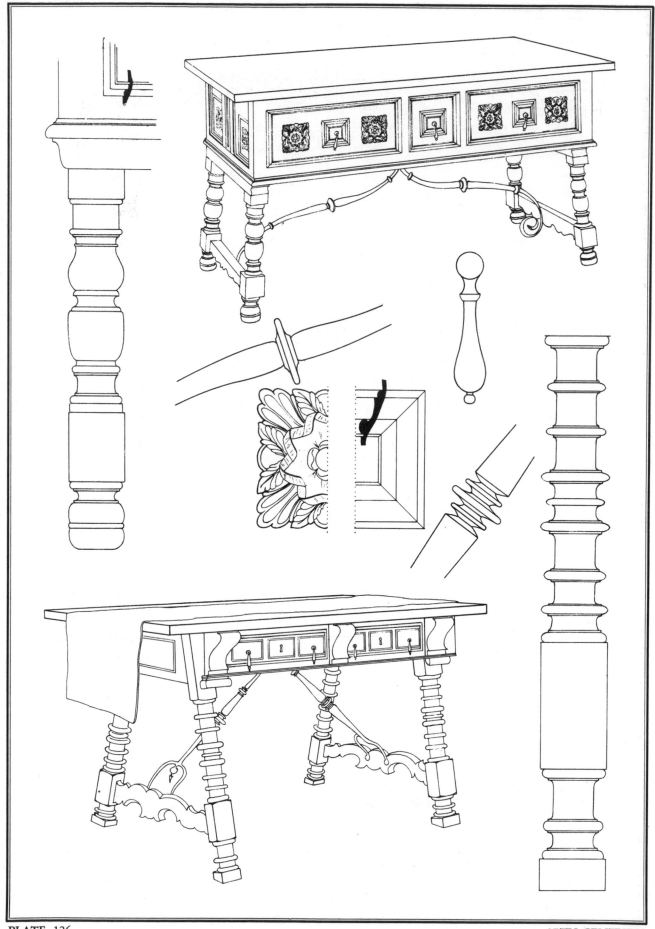

PLATE 126
Tables with turned legs in form of pyramid with wrought-iron crosspieces.

17TH CENTURY

Tavera Hospital, Toledo

PLATE 127
Tables with turned legs and decorative baroque carvings on front.

PLATE 128
Tables with turned legs and decorative baroque carvings on front.

Museum of Decorative Arts, Madrid

PLATE 129

Tables with turned legs and decorative baroque carvings on front.

17TH CENTURY

Museum of Decorative Arts, Madrid

PLATE 130

Small tables with turned legs and decorative baroque carvings on the front.

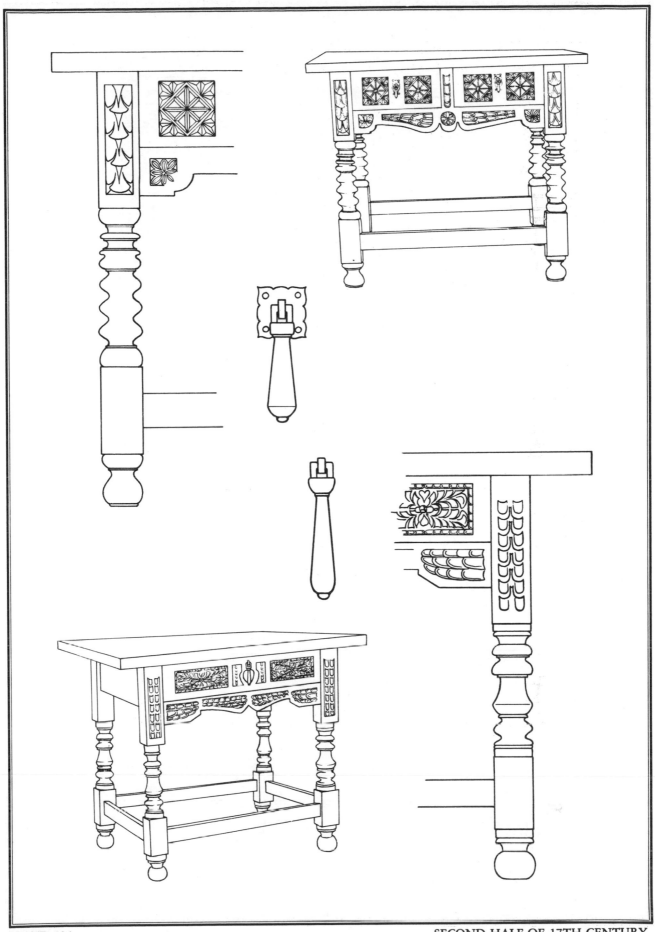

PLATE 131
Small tables with decorative carvings in folk motifs.

SECOND HALF OF 17TH CENTURY

Private collection

PLATE 132
Small tables with decorative carvings in folk motifs.

Private collection

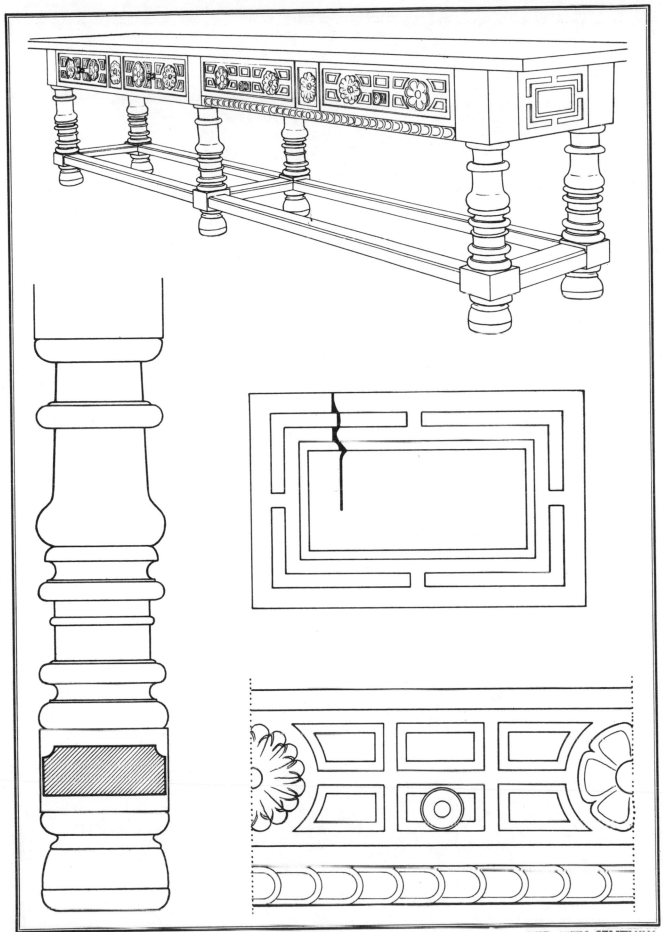

PLATE 133
Table-counter decorated with baroque carvings on the front.

Private collection

PLATE 134
Table decorated with baroque carvings.

Museum of Decorative Arts, Madrid

PLATE 135
Tables with drawers decorated with moulding and carvings.

Museum of Decorative Arts, Madrid

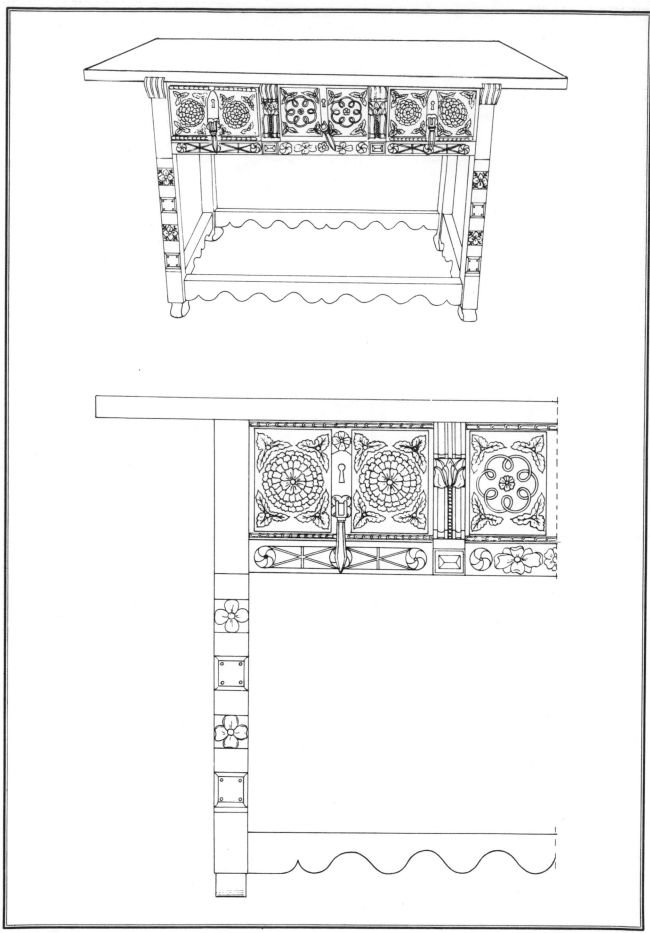

PLATE 136
Table decorated with folk carvings.

17TH CENTURY

Museum of Decorative Arts, Madrid

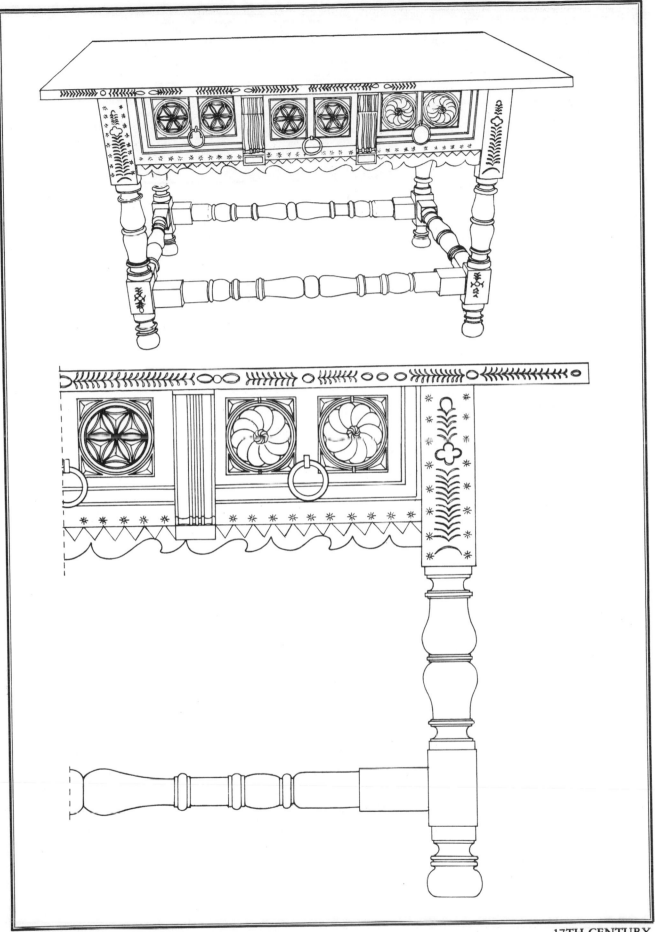

PLATE 137
Table decorated with folk carvings.

Museum of Decorative Arts, Madrid

PLATE 138
Tables decorated with folk carvings.

Museum of Decorative Arts, Madrid

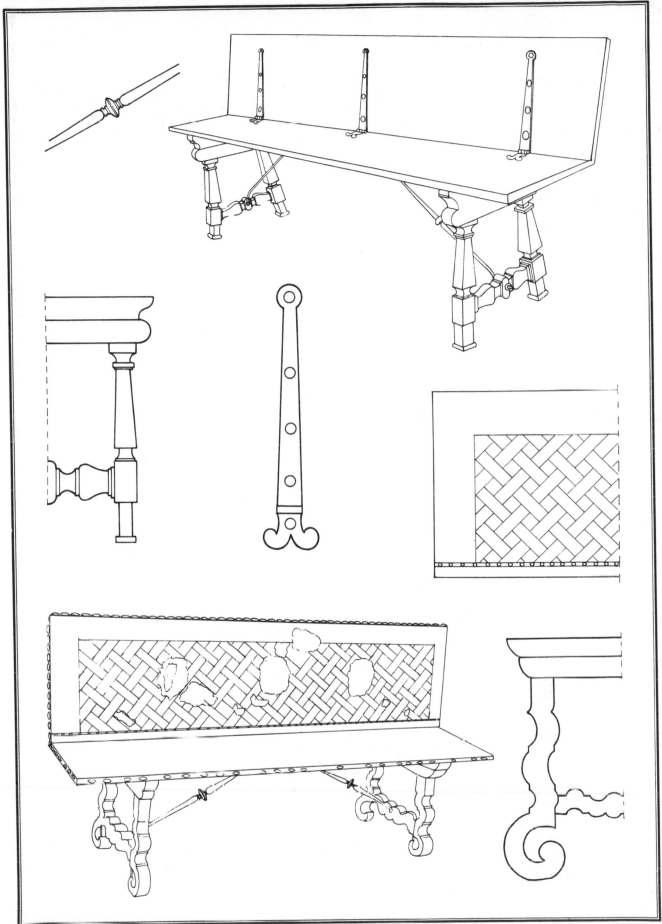

PLATE 139
Bench with wrought-iron hinges and crosspieces. Bench with a braided leather back, cut legs and wrought-iron crosspieces.
Museum of Decorative Arts and National Archeological Museum, Madrid

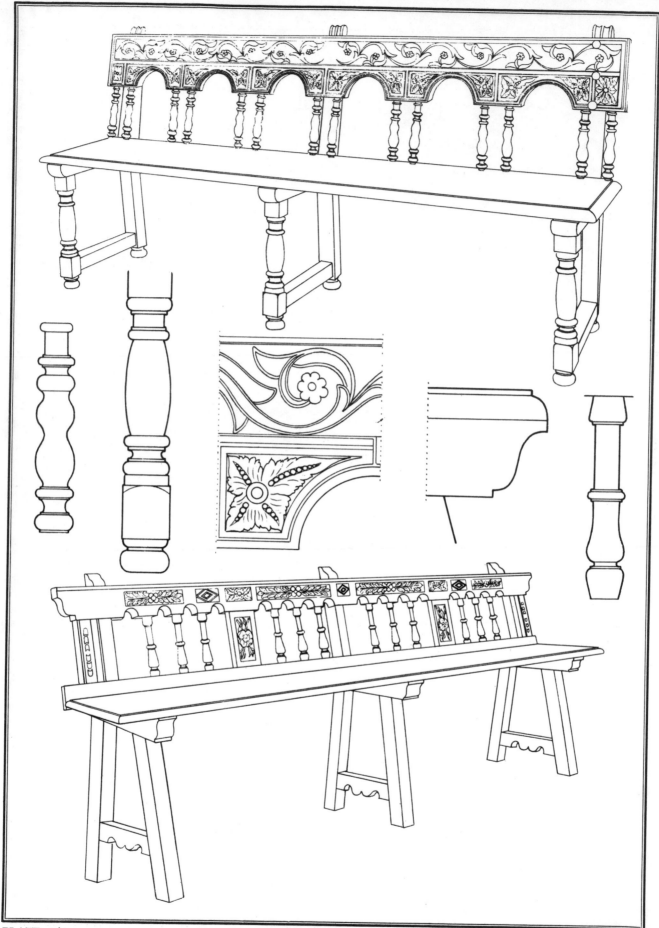

PLATE 140
Bench with "bridge" back and turned legs. Bench with "bridge" back.

Private collection and Parador of Gredos, Avila

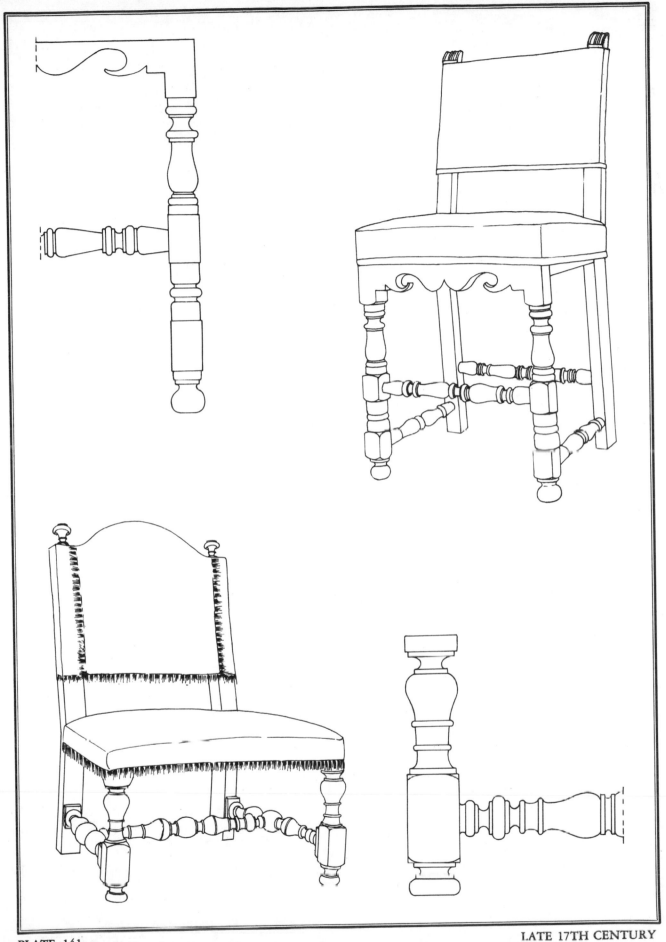

PLATE 141
Cloth-trimmed chairs with turned legs.

Gustavo Gili collection, Santillana del Mar

PLATE 142

Cloth-trimmed chair decorated with geometric motifs on front. Friar's armchair trimmed with leather and gilt metal nails.

Gustavo Gili collection, Santillana del Mar

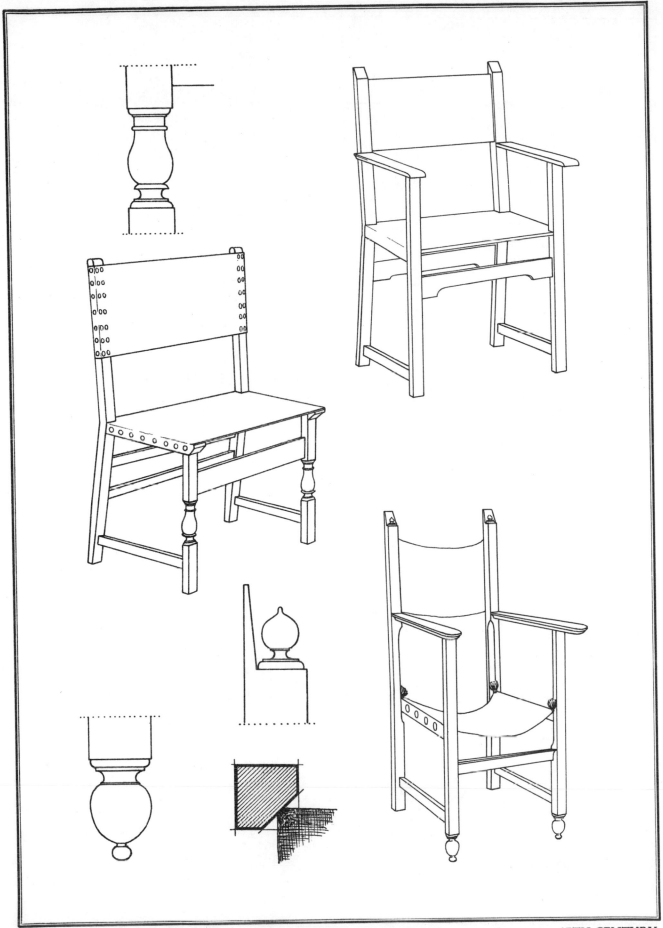

PLATE 143
Friars' armchairs and chair trimmed with leather and gilt metal nails.

PLATE 144   17TH CENTURY
Chair with multicolored, embossed leather back. Chair trimmed with leather and gilt metal nails.

Museum of Decorative Arts, Madrid

PLATE 145
Friars' armchairs trimmed with cloth and openwork fronts.

17TH CENTURY

Museum of Decorative Arts, Madrid

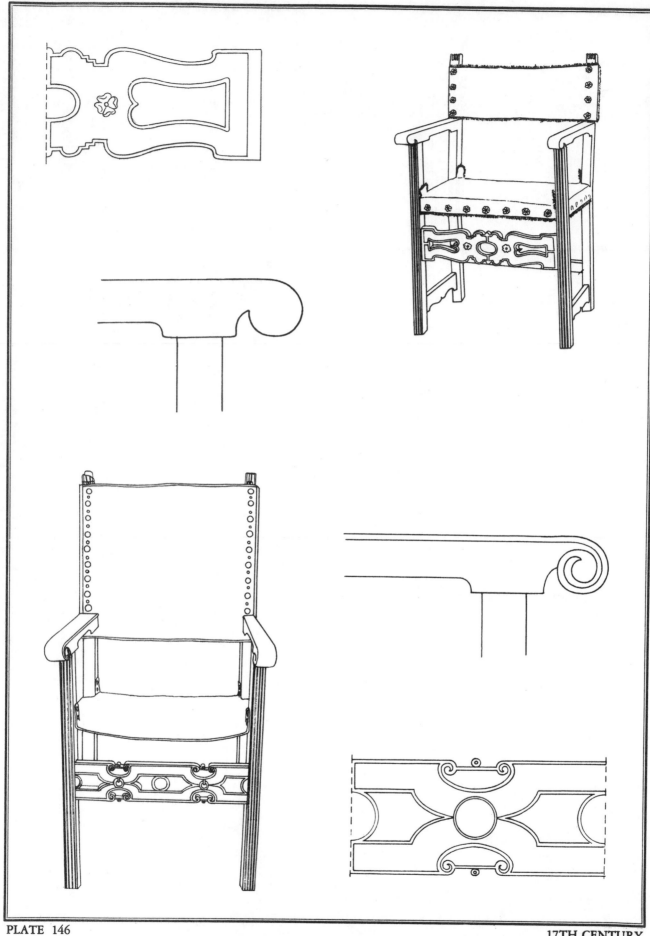

PLATE 146
Friars' armchairs with openwork front, trimmed with leather and gilt nails.

17TH CENTURY

Museum of Decorative Arts, Madrid

PLATE 147

17TH CENTURY

Friars' armchairs. The lower one has carved brackets supporting the arms, round finials and ornate gilt metal nails, and is from El Greco's house in Toledo.

Upper chair: Parador of Gredos, Avila

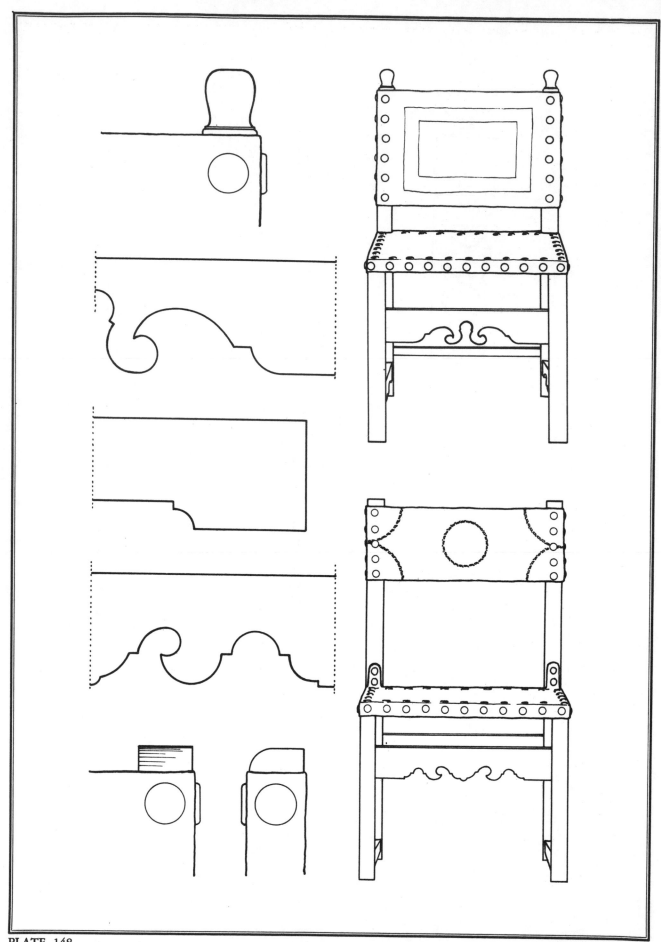

PLATE 148

17TH CENTURY

Chairs trimmed with leather with cut-wooden crosspieces and gilt metal nails.

PLATE 149
Chair and armchair trimmed with cloth, with gilt metal nails and decorated with baroque carvings.

17TH CENTURY

Private collection

PLATE 150

Friars' armchairs. The upper one is trimmed with leather and has an openwork crosspiece; the lower one is trimmed with cloth and has a carved crosspiece.

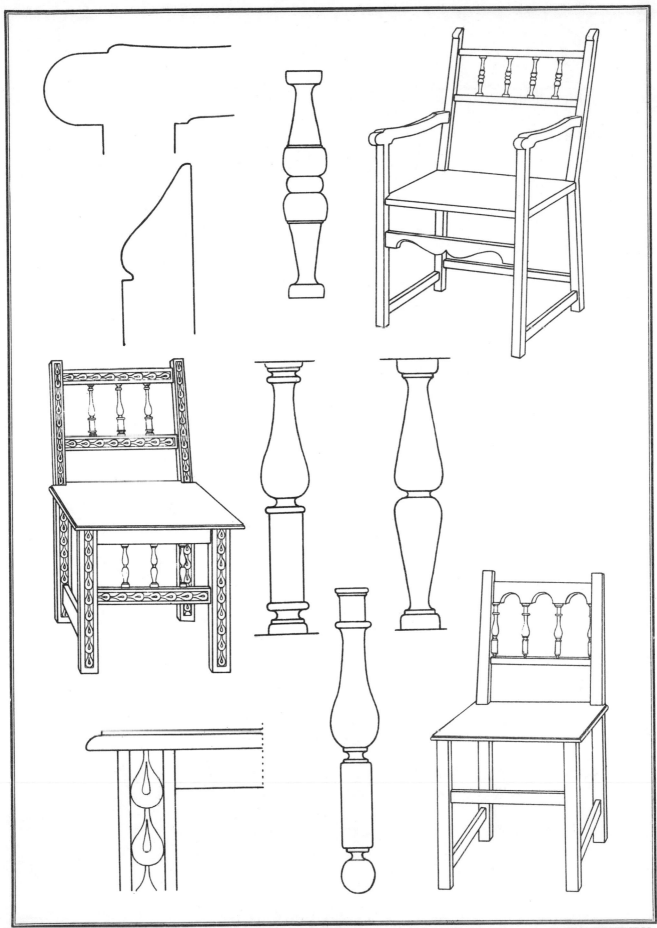

PLATE 151

PLATE 151
Chairs and armchair in folk style with backs of turned balusters.

17TH CENTURY

155

PLATE 152
Cloth-trimmed armchairs with "table" arms and carved openwork crosspieces.

Riudabell Castle

PLATE 153

High-backed chairs of Central European style trimmed with engraved leather, turned legs and openwork crosspieces.

Lower chair: Museum of Decorative Arts, Madrid

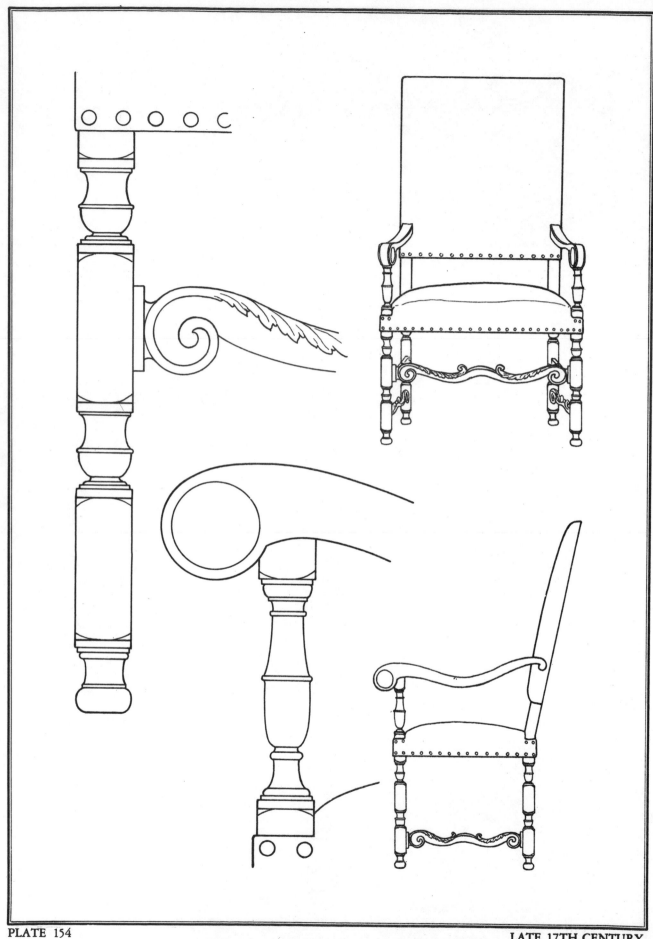

PLATE 154
High-backed armchair of Central European style, trimmed with cloth, and with turned legs.

Babra Arroyos collection

PLATE 155   LATE 17TH CENTURY

High-backed chair and armchair of Central European style, trimmed with cloth, and with openwork crosspieces.

Palace of the Counts of Perelada, Palma de Mallorca

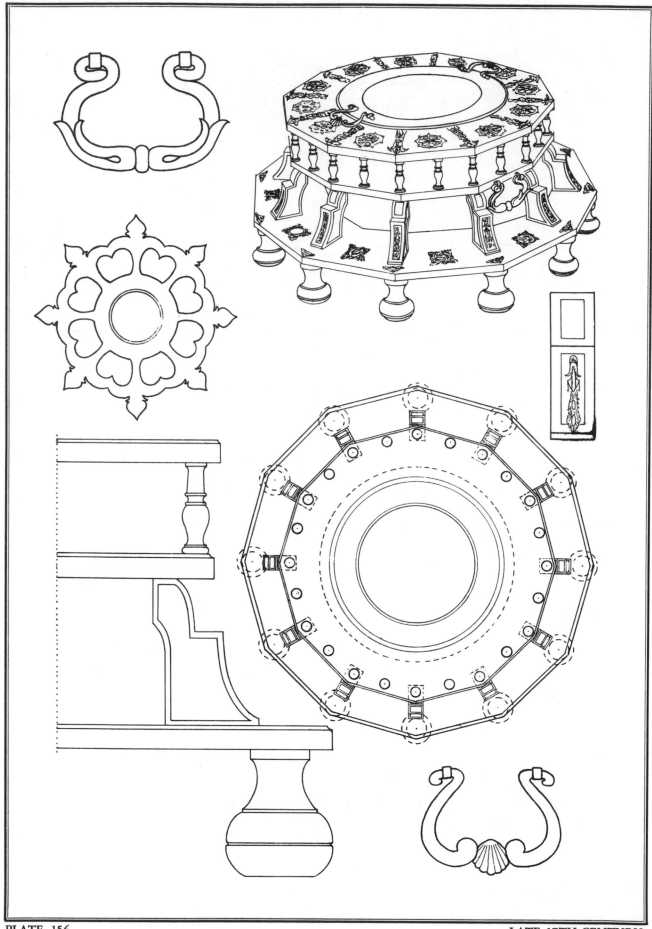

PLATE 156
Three-piece brazier decorated with carvings and copper nails.

LATE 17TH CENTURY

Tavera Hospital, Toledo

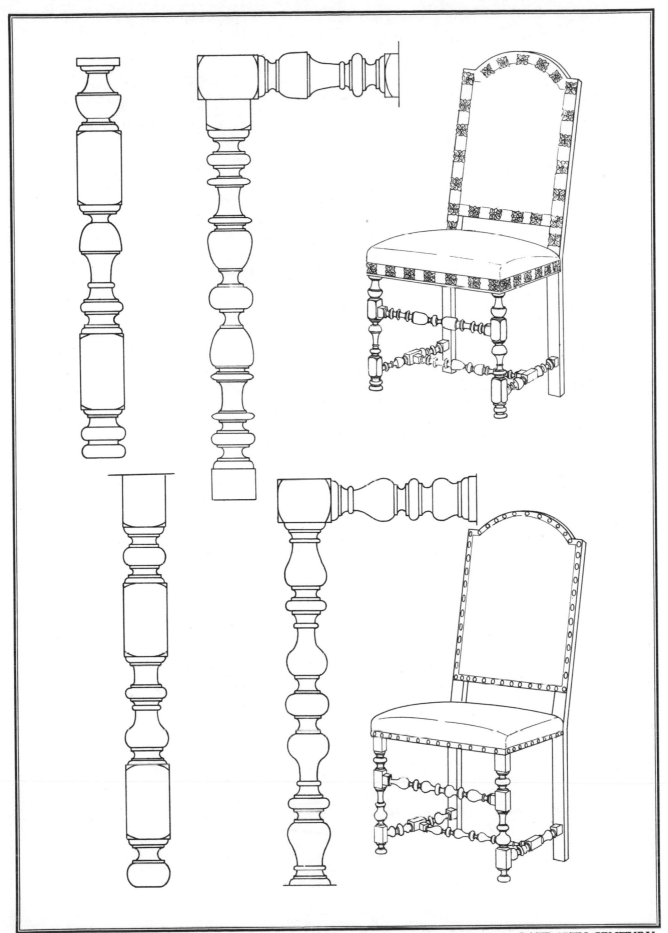

PLATE 157   LATE 17TH CENTURY
Central European style of chairs with high backs, turned legs, and trimmed with cloth and gilt metal nails.

House of the Marquis of Campofranco and Casa Olaya, Palma de Mallorca

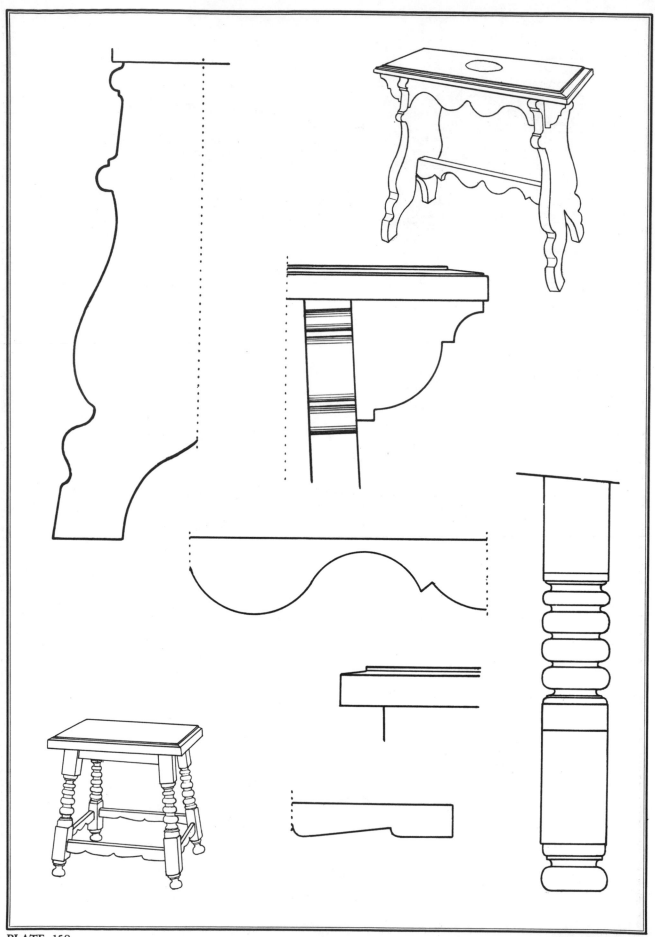

PLATE 158
Wooden benches with cut or turned legs.

17TH CENTURY

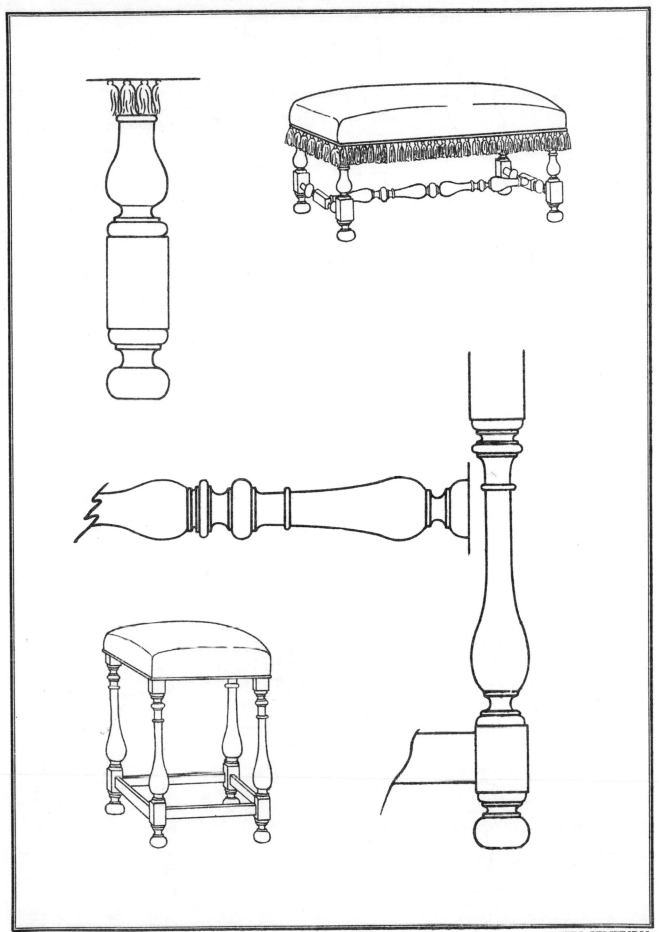

PLATE 159
Benches with cloth trimming and turned legs.

17TH CENTURY

Casa de las Dueñas, Seville

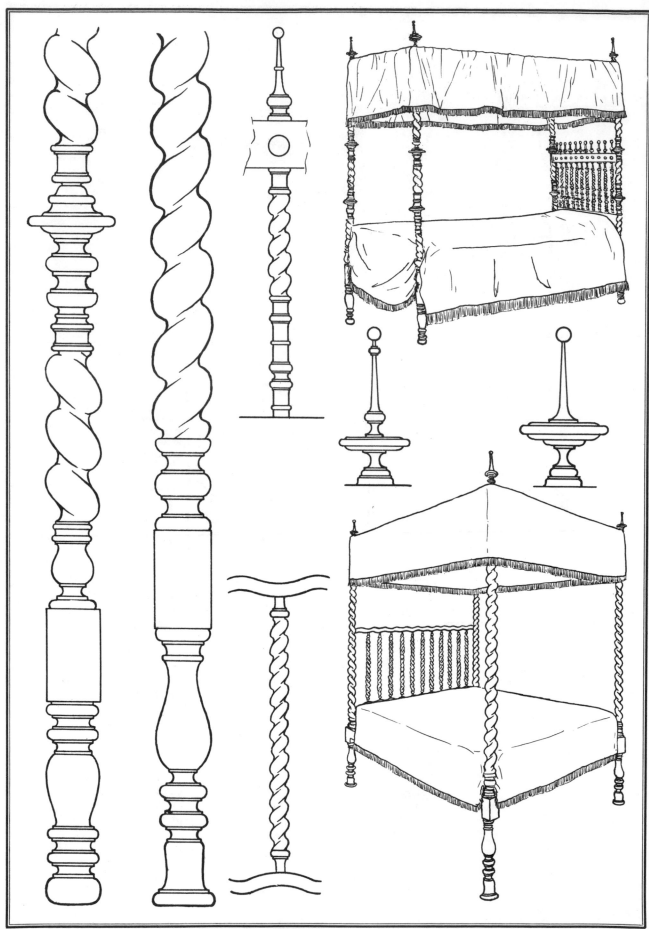

PLATE 160

Beds with canopies and valances. Turned posts and balusters in form of twisted columns.

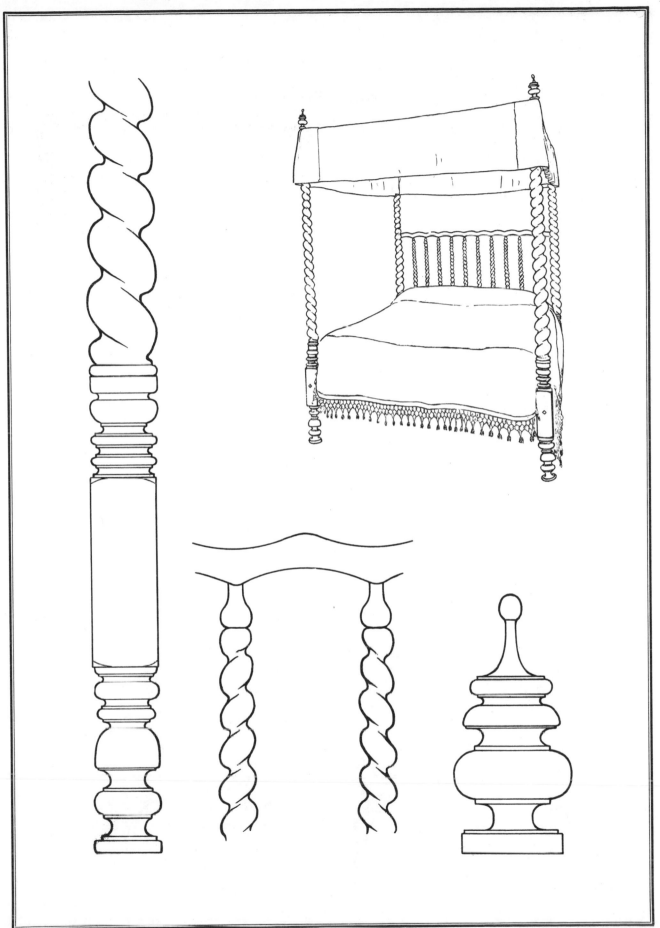

PLATE 161

Bed with canopy and valance. Turned posts and balusters in form of twisted columns.

Barcelona

PLATE 162
Turned and carved wooden bed.

LATE 17TH CENTURY

PLATE 163

LATE 17TH CENTURY

Portuguese-style bed of foreign woods, with gilt metal decorations. Posts and balusters of back were worked on a lathe.

Mrs. Anton Matheus collection

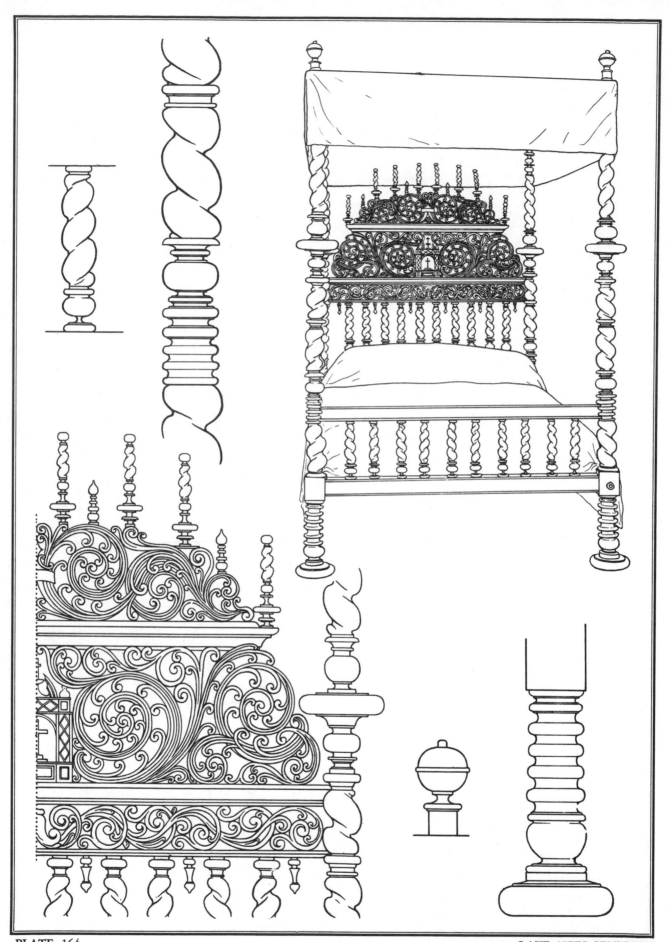

PLATE 164

LATE 17TH CENTURY

Portuguese bed. Turned posts and balusters in form of twisted columns. Gilt metal decorations.

Richard Blanco collection, Santiago de Compostela

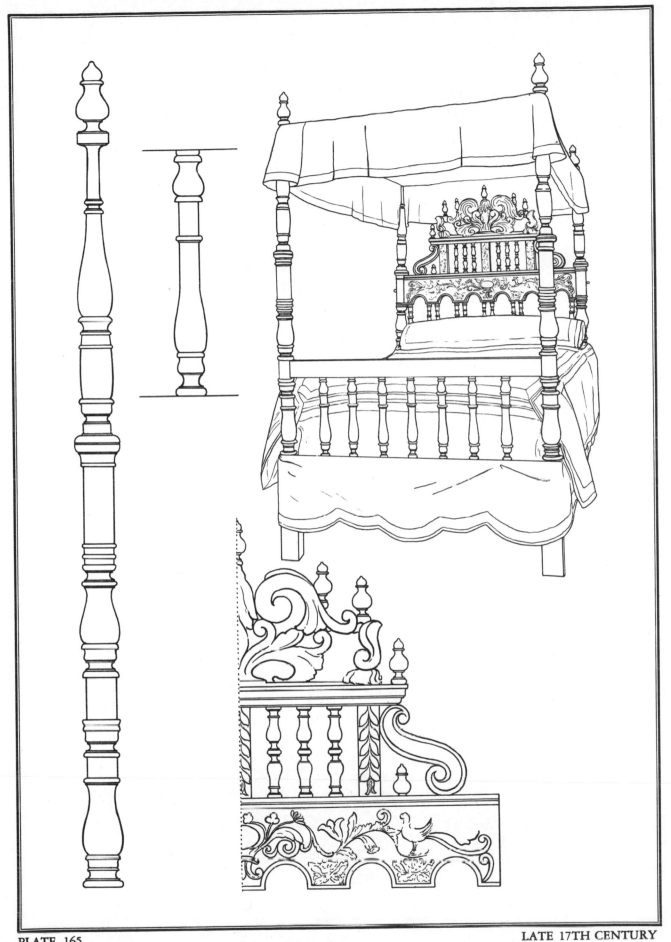

PLATE 165
Portuguese-style bed. Posts, headboard and footboard of turned wood. Gilt metal decorations.

Beancharro collection, Pontevedra

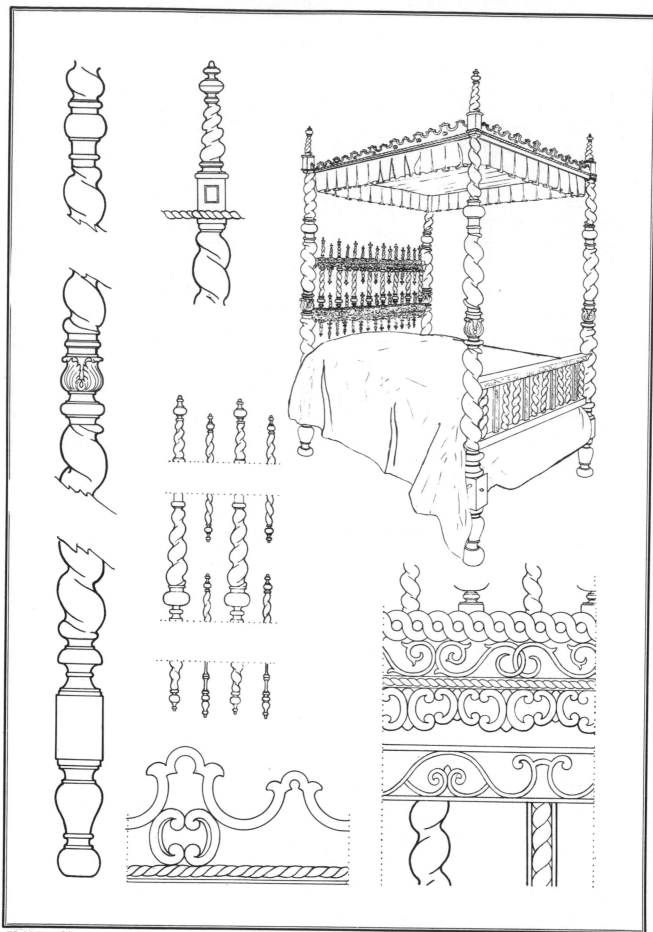

PLATE 166

LATE 17TH CENTURY

Portuguese bed with canopy and valance. Posts and balusters in form of twisted columns. Gilt metal decorations.

Canet de Mar, Barcelona

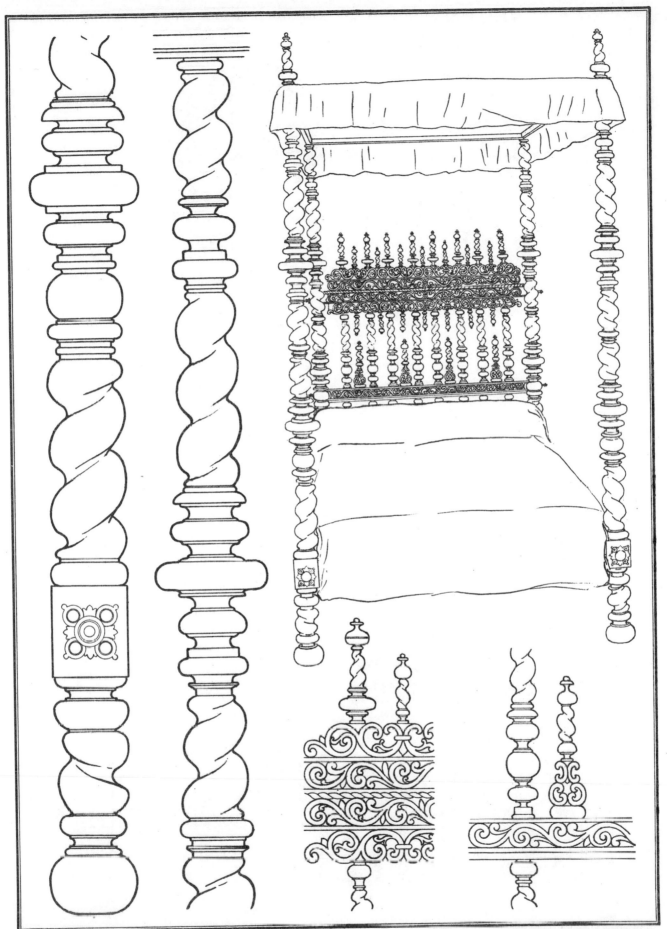

PLATE 167

Portuguese bed with canopy and valance. Posts and balusters are in the form of twisted columns. Gilt metal decorations.

Solsona, Lerida

PLATE 168
Portuguese bed of ebony with gilt metal decorations.

Museum of Decorative Arts, Madrid

PLATE 169
Portuguese bed of ebony with twisted posts. Openwork cornice and gilt metal decorations.

Museum of Decorative Arts, Madrid

PLATE 170
Braziers with decorative copper nails and engraved copper handles.

17TH CENTURY

National Archeological Museum, Madrid

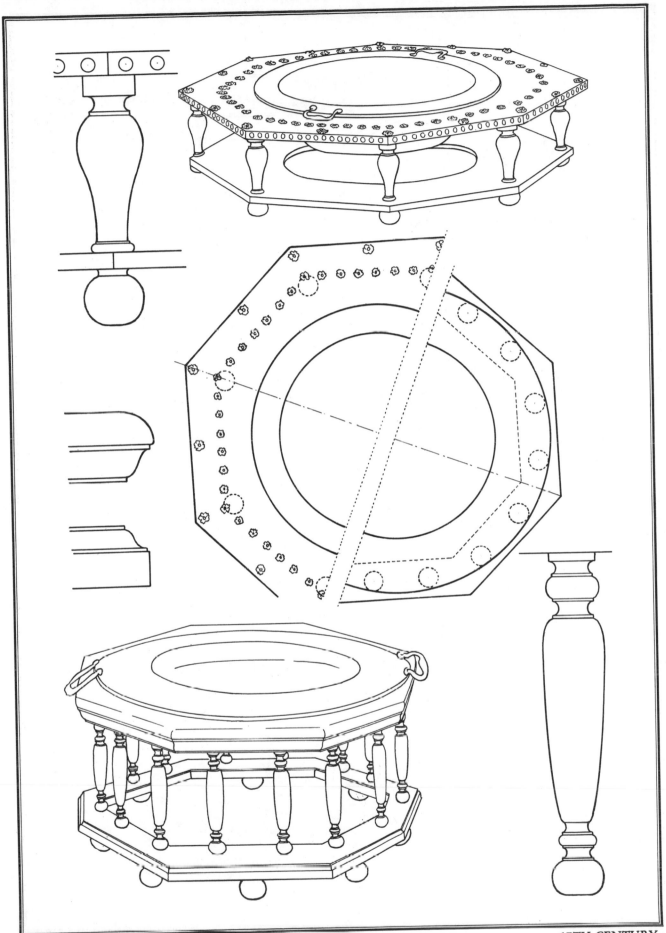

PLATE 171
Braziers supported by balusters and decorated with copper nails.

PLATE 172
Braziers. The lower one is decorated with baroque pictures.

Tavera Hospital, Toledo

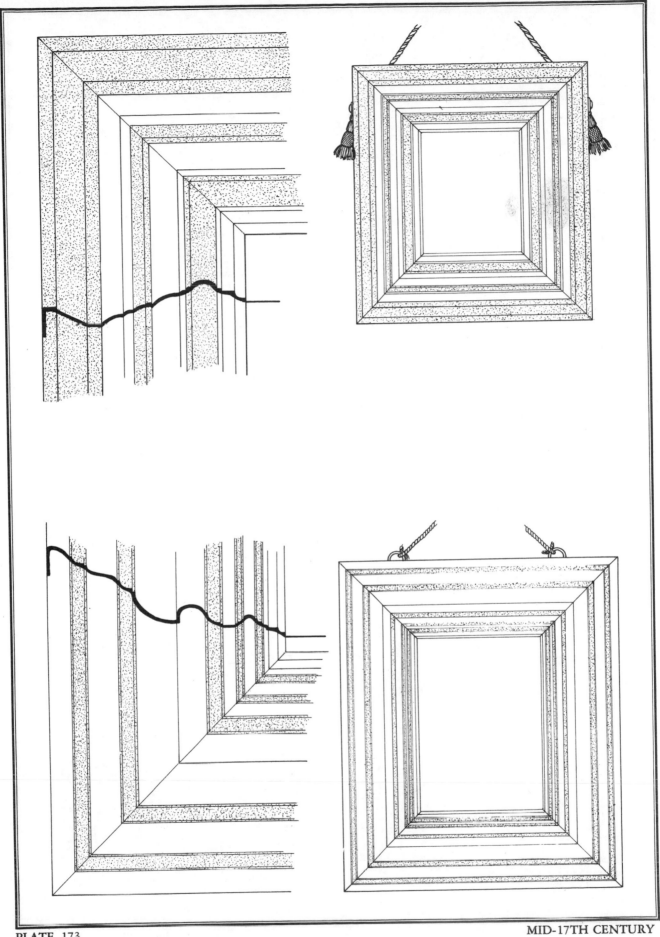

PLATE 173
Mirror frames of ebony moulding.

MID-17TH CENTURY

Lope de Vega's house, Madrid

PLATE 174
Picture frames decorated with baroque carvings in corners and centers.

SECOND HALF OF 17TH CENTURY

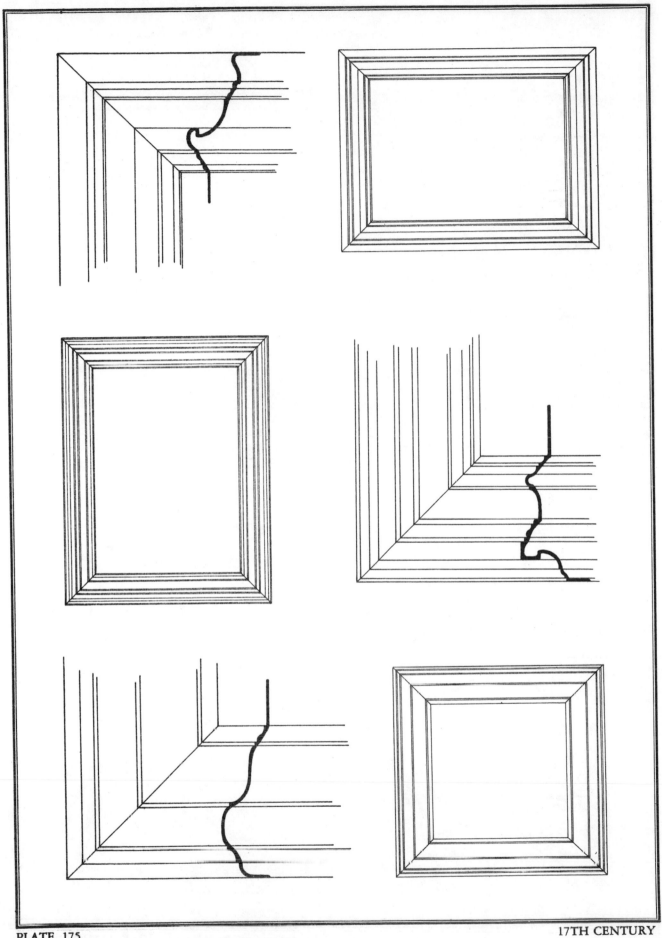

PLATE 175
Picture or mirror frames of moulded wood painted black.
Museum of Paintings, Bilbao; Romantic Museum and Fundaciones Vega Inclán, Madrid and Parador of Merida, Badajoz

PLATE 176
Picture frames decorated with baroque carvings.

SECOND HALF OF 17TH CENTURY

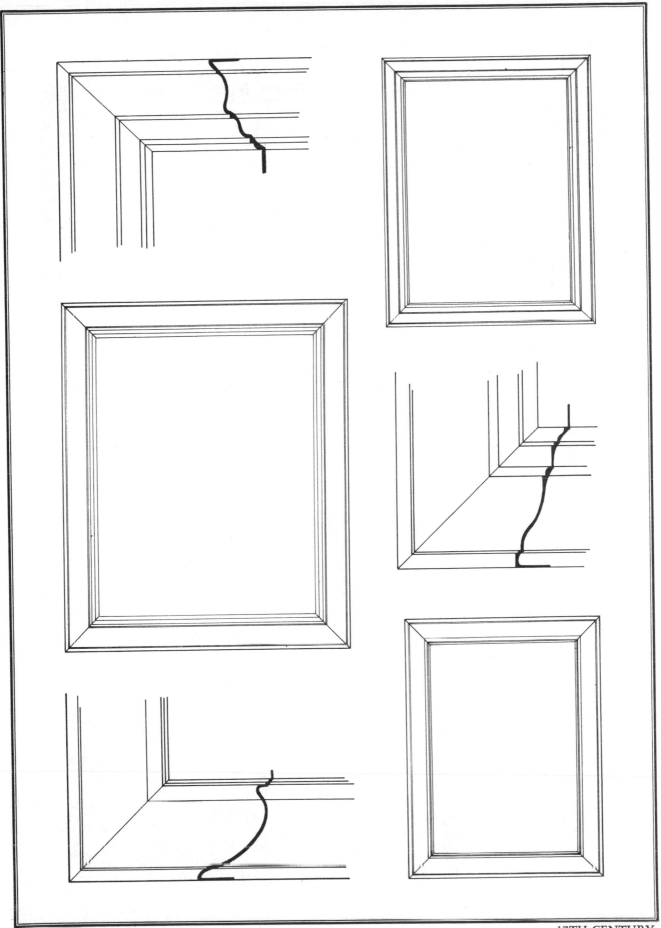

PLATE 177   17TH CENTURY
Frames of moulded wood painted black.
Romantic Museum, Fundaciones Vega Inclán and Lope de Vega's house, Madrid and Museum of Painting, Seville

PLATE 179
Brass candle holders.

SECOND HALF OF 17TH CENTURY

Lope de Vega's house, Madrid

PLATE 180
Large Mudejar-style chest.

Grases collection, Barcelona

PLATE 181
Large folk-style chest.

17TH CENTURY

Museum of Decorative Arts, Madrid

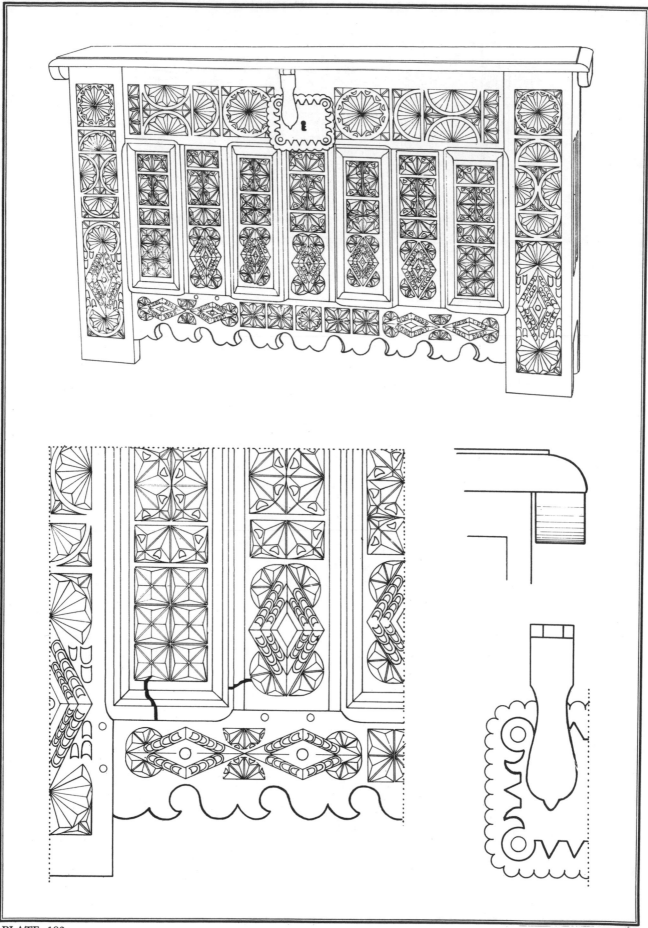

PLATE 182
Large Mudejar-style chest.

Gazolaz Parochial Church, Navarre

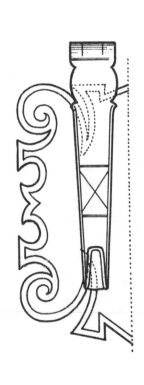

PLATE 183
Large folk-style chest.

Marquis de la Torre collection, Palma de Mallorca

PLATE 184
Chest in folk design.

17TH CENTURY

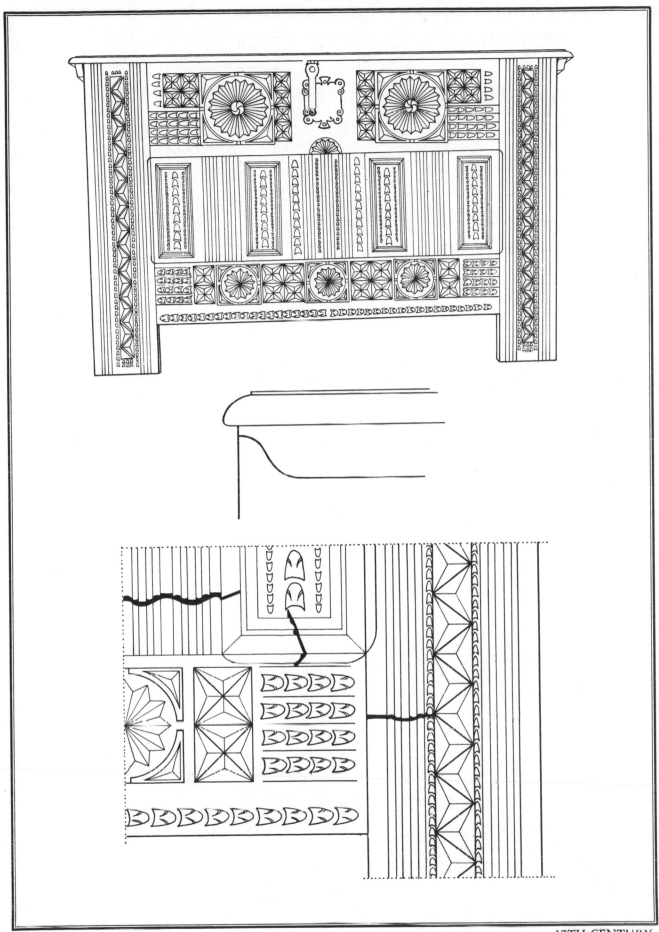

PLATE 185
Large folk-style chest.

PLATE 186
Large chest.

17TH CENTURY

190

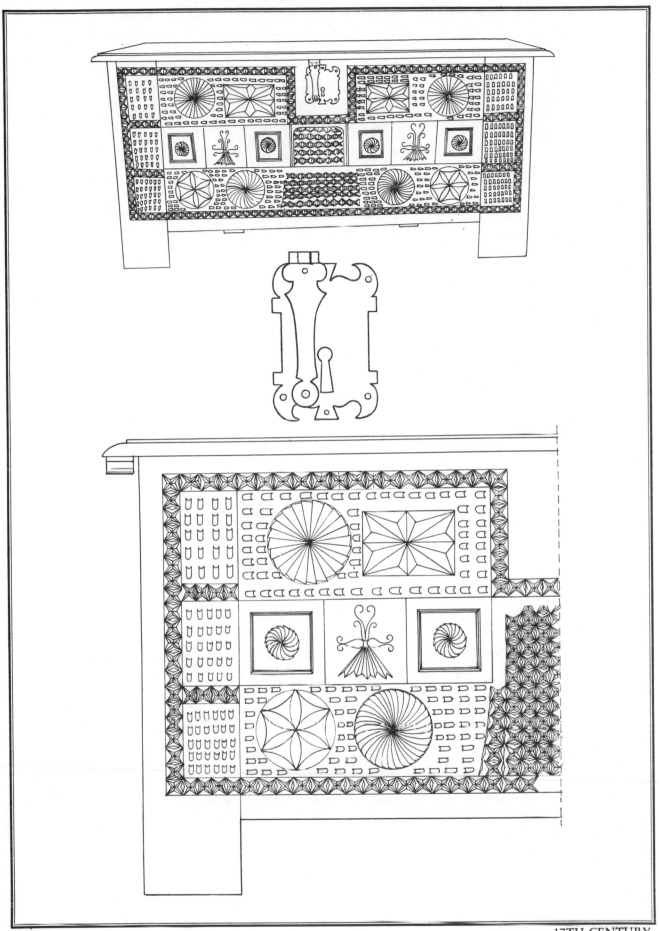

PLATE 187
Folk-style chest.

17TH CENTURY

Museum of Decorative Arts, Madrid

PLATE 188
Large chests.

National Museum of Decorative Arts, Madrid

PLATE 190
Folk-style chest.

17TH CENTURY

Museum of Decorative Arts, Madrid

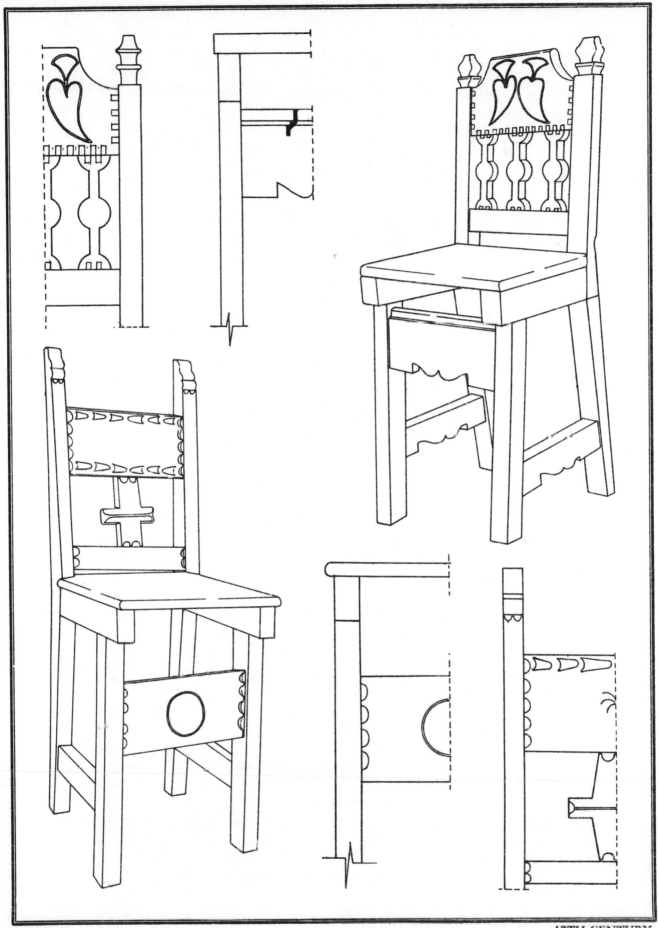

PLATE 191
Chairs of folk design.

Gustavo Gili collection, Santillana del Mar

PLATE 192
Folk-style chest.

Museum of Decorative Arts, Madrid

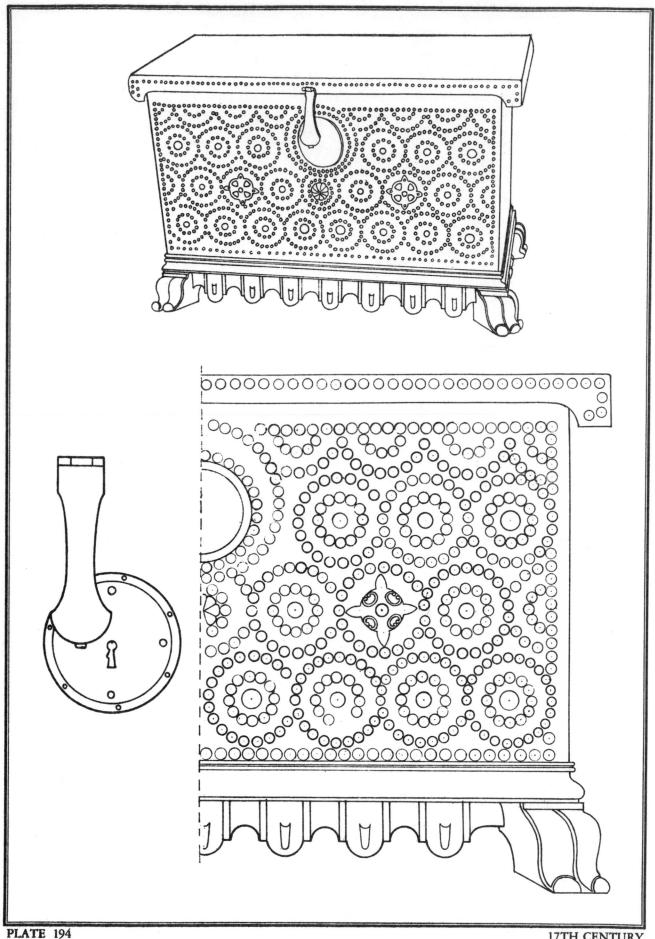

PLATE 194
Chest covered with leather and decorative nails.

Museum of Decorative Arts, Madrid

PLATE 195
Folk-style cupboard.

17TH CENTURY

199

PLATE 196
Chest-on-chest.

El Greco's house, Toledo

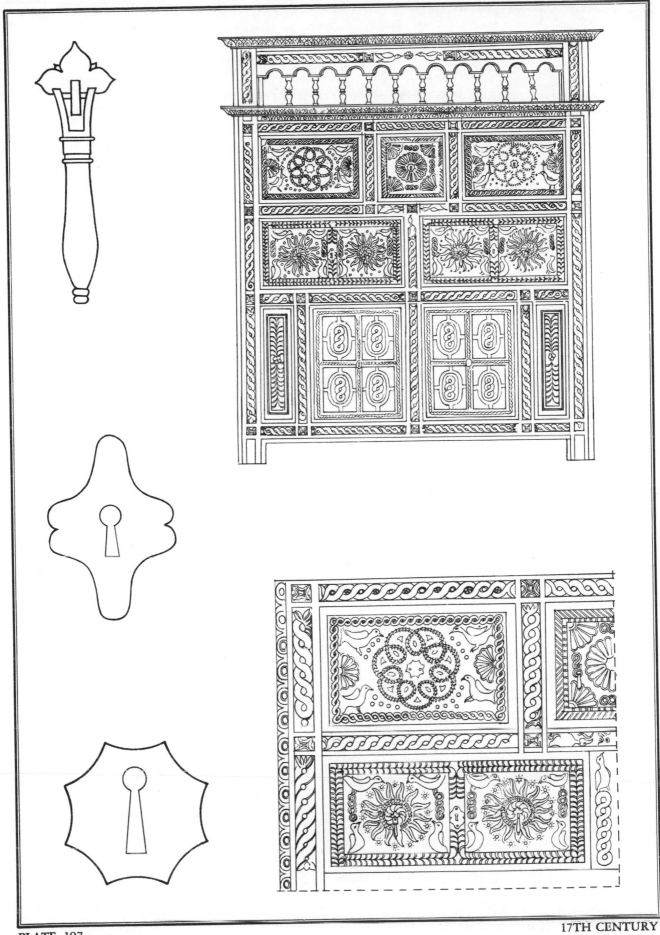

PLATE 197
Carved wardrobe of folk design.

Museum of Decorative Arts, Madrid

PLATE 198
Bench with decorative carvings.

Private collection

PLATE 199
Bench decorated with folk art carvings.

Private collection

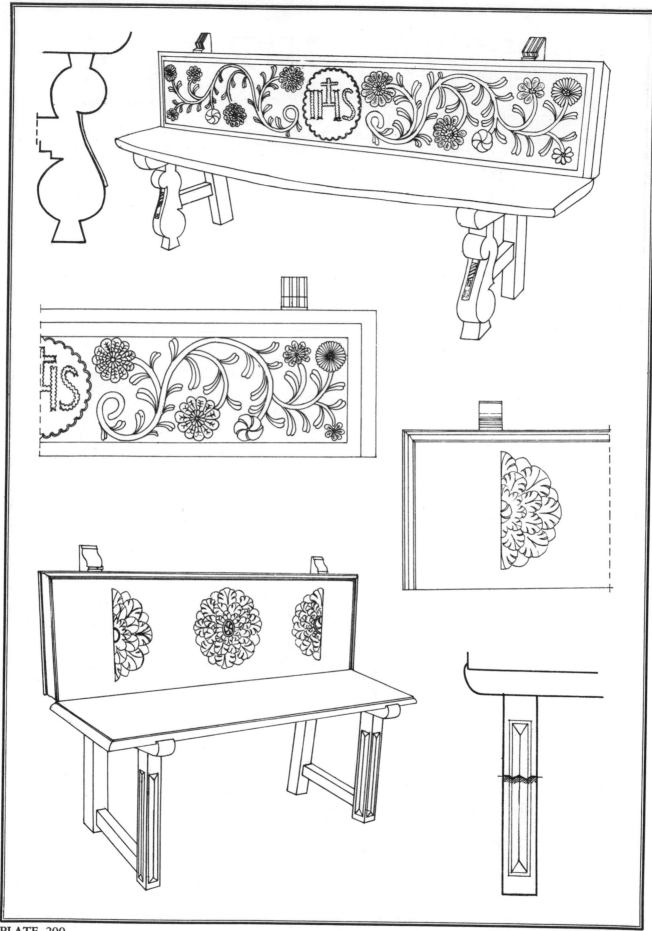

PLATE 200
Folk-style benches with decorative carvings.

Museum of Decorative Arts, Madrid

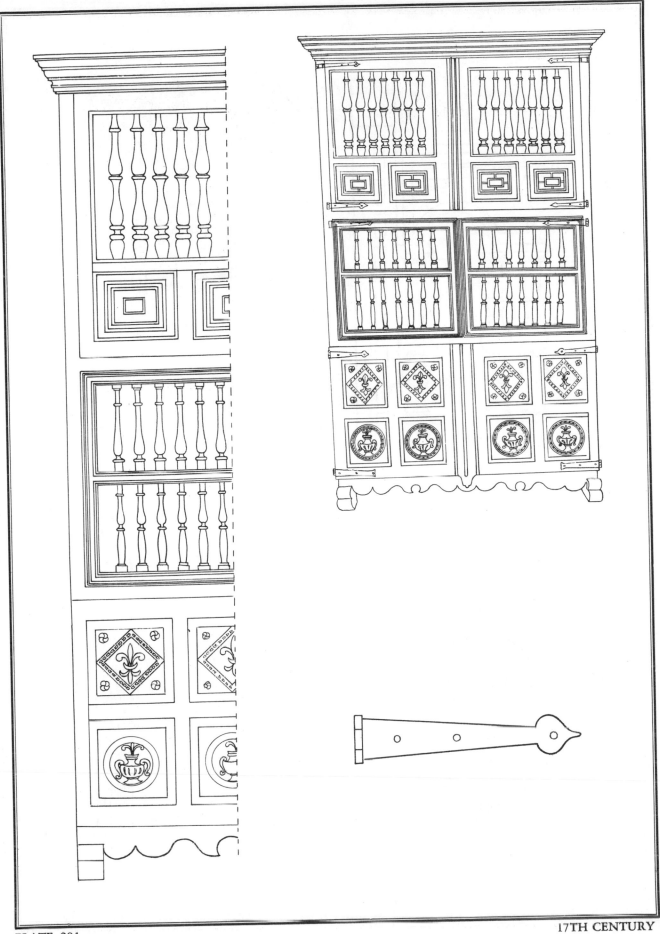

PLATE 201
Folk-style wardrobe.

Museum of Decorative Arts, Madrid

PLATE 202
Folk-style chairs.

17TH CENTURY

206

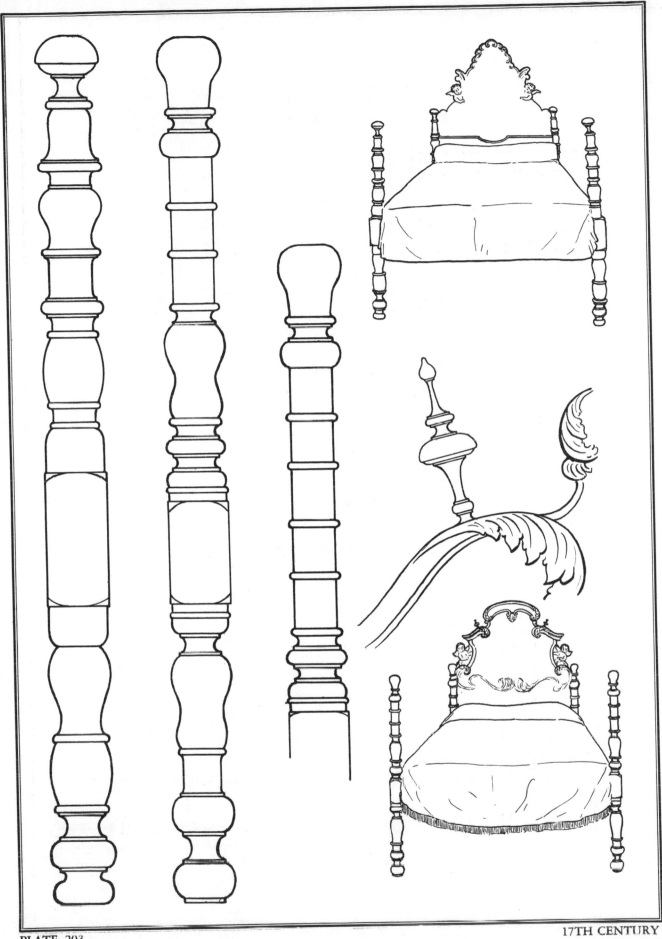

PLATE 203
Beds of folk design.

PLATE 204
Table with folding leaves.

SECOND HALF OF 17TH CENTURY

Museum of Decorative Arts, Madrid

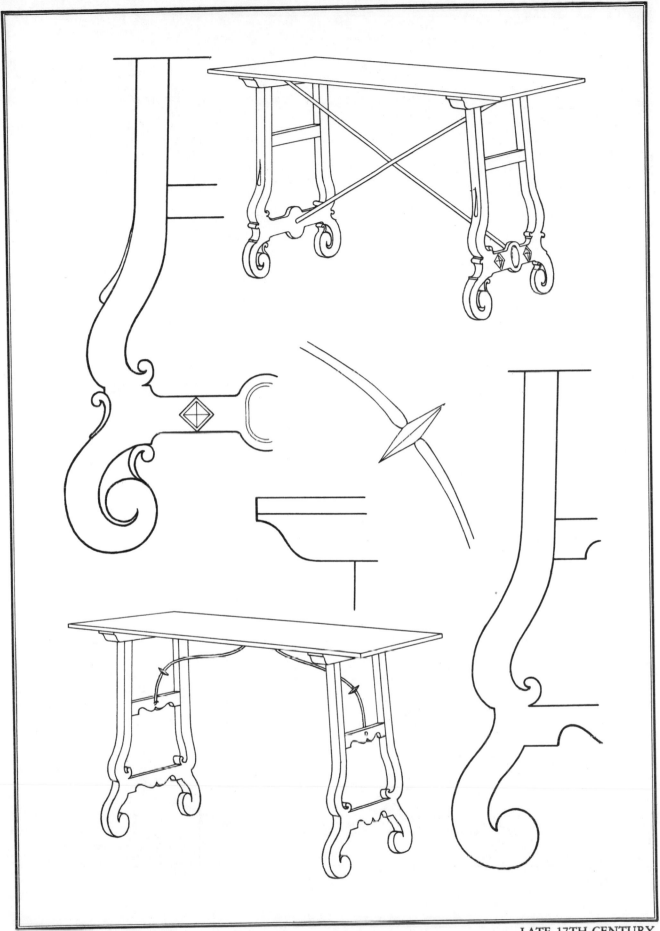

PLATE 205
Two tables.

Museum of Pontevedra and the Parador of Santillana del Mar

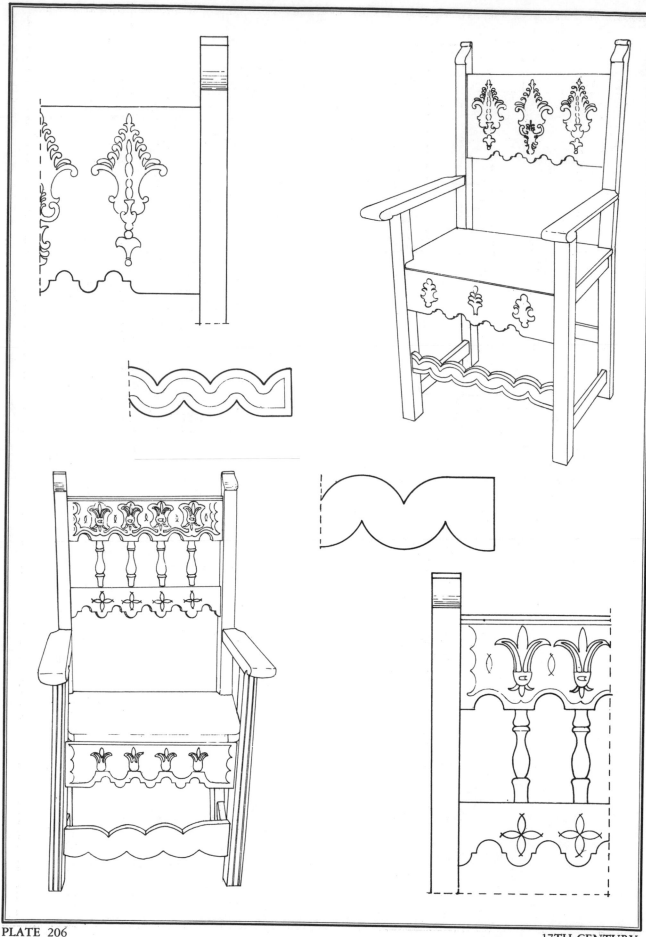

PLATE 206
Folk-style armchairs.

17TH CENTURY

Museum of Decorative Arts, Madrid

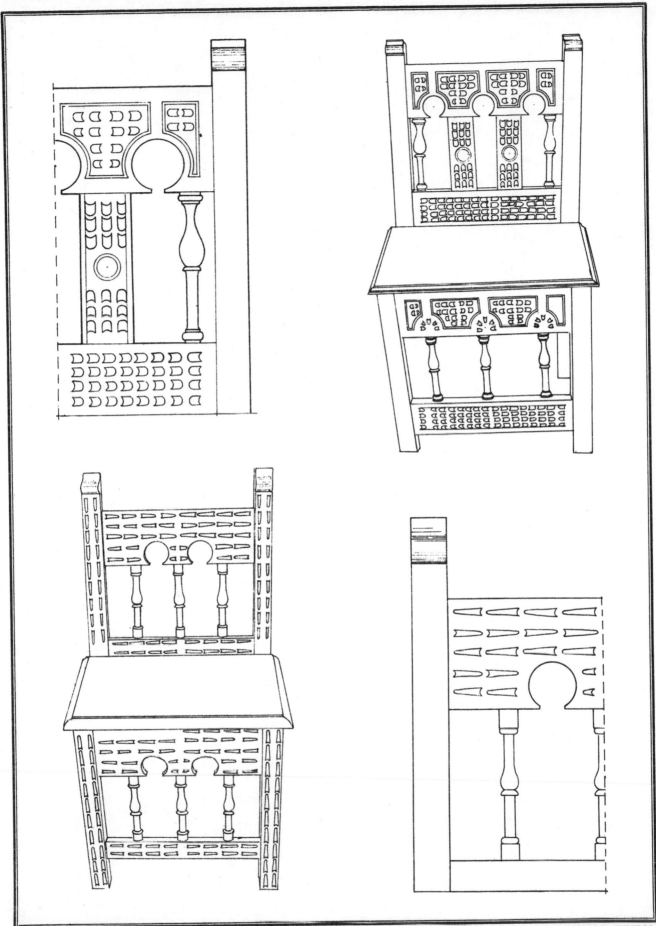

PLATE 207
Folk-style chairs.

Museum of Decorative Arts, Madrid

PLATE 208
Chairs of folk design.

Gustavo Gili collection, Santillana del Mar

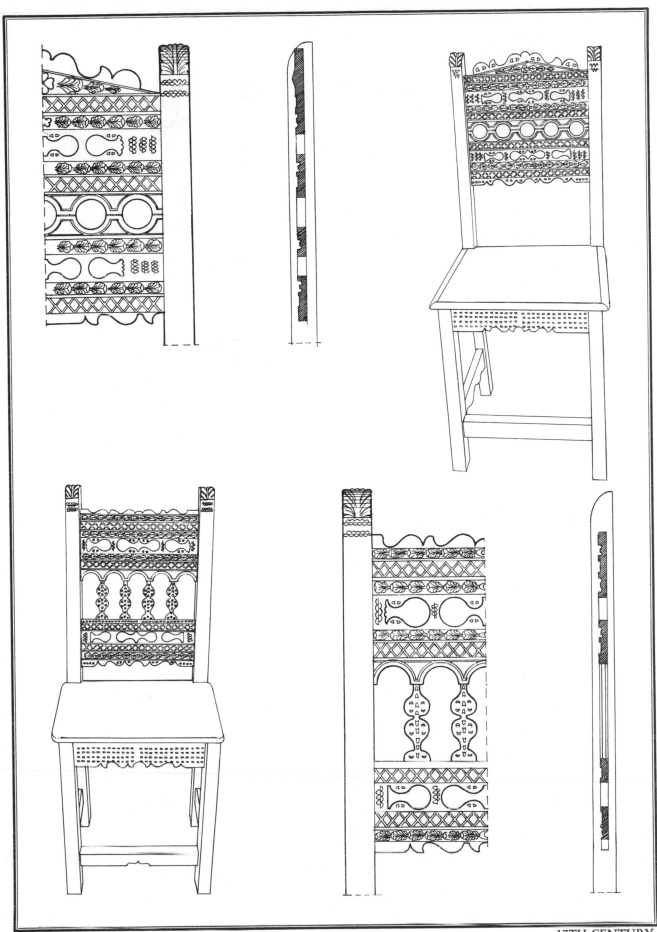

PLATE 209
Folk-style chairs.

Museum of Decorative Arts, Madrid

PLATE 211
Folk-style chairs.

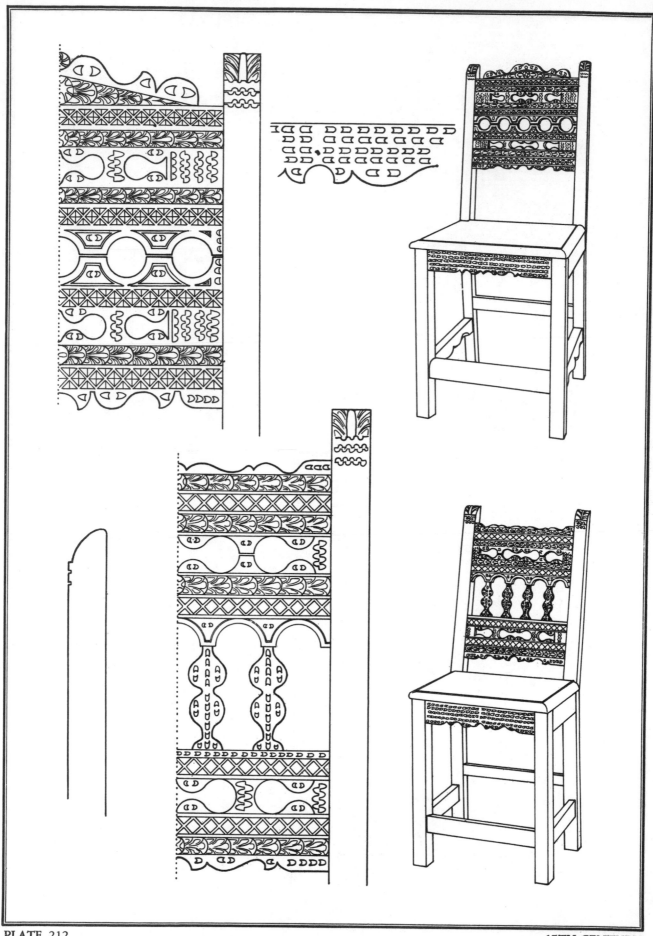

PLATE 212
Folk-style chairs.

17TH CENTURY

216

PLATE 213
Folk-style chairs.

PLATE 214
Folk-style chairs.

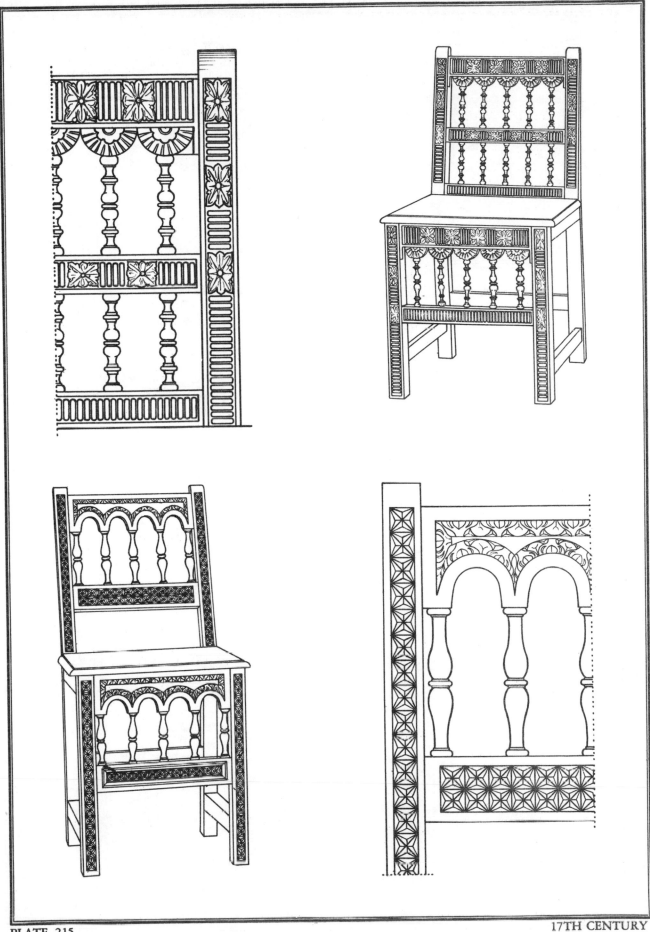

PLATE 215
Folk-style chairs.

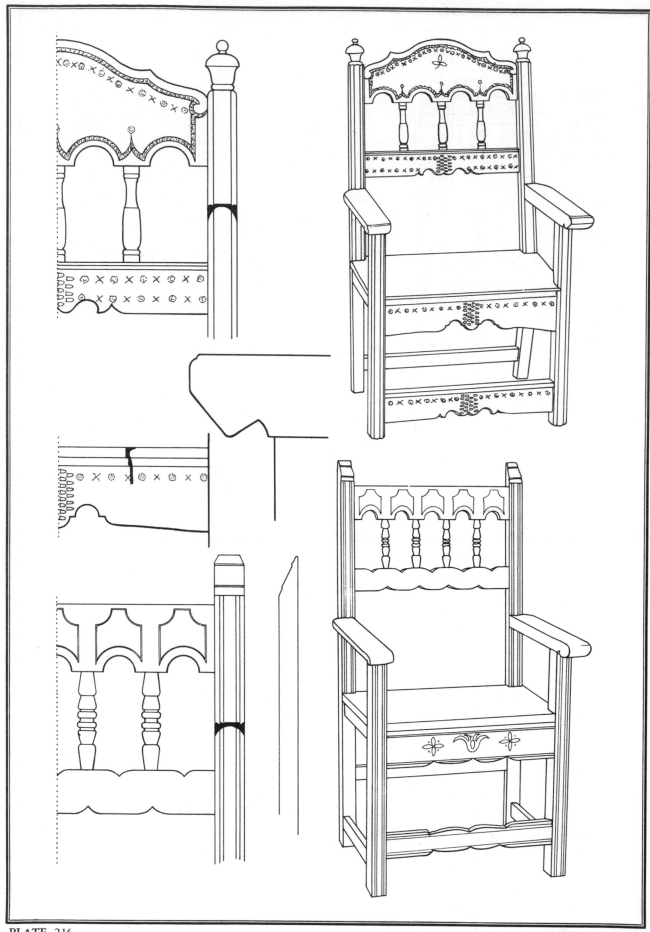

PLATE 216
Folk-style chairs.

Tavera Hospital, Toledo

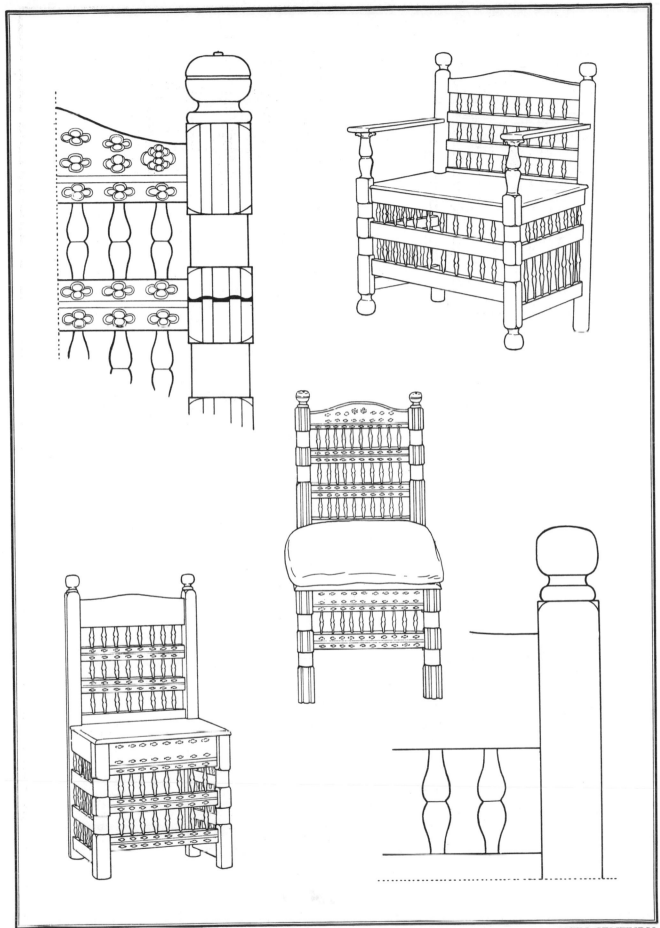

PLATE 217
Folk-style chairs.

PLATE 218
Folk-style chairs.

National Museum of Decorative Arts and Hostería del Estudiante, Alcalá de Henares

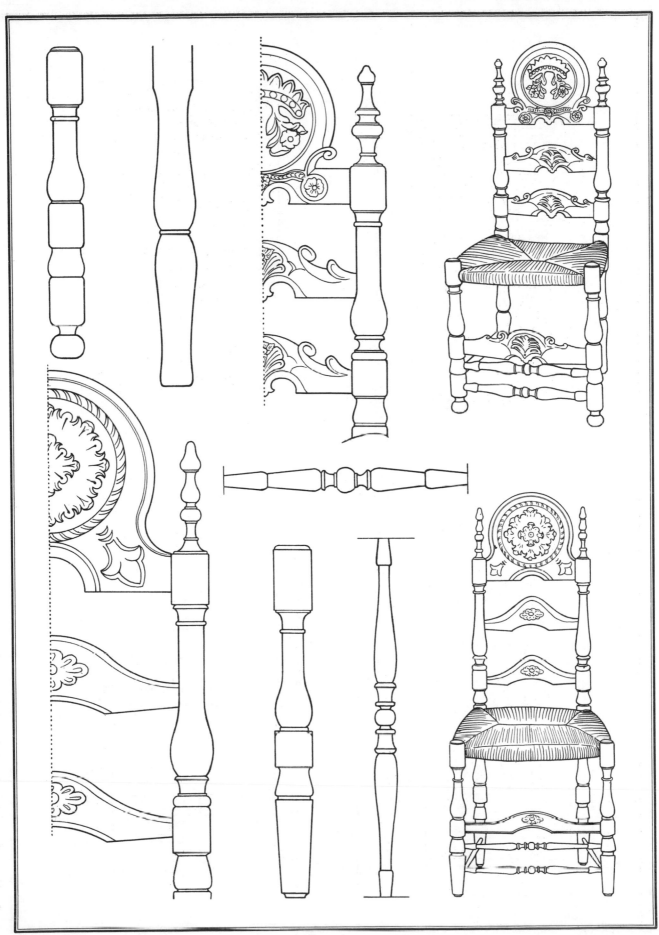

PLATE 219
Chairs of folk design.

Francisco Fábregas collection

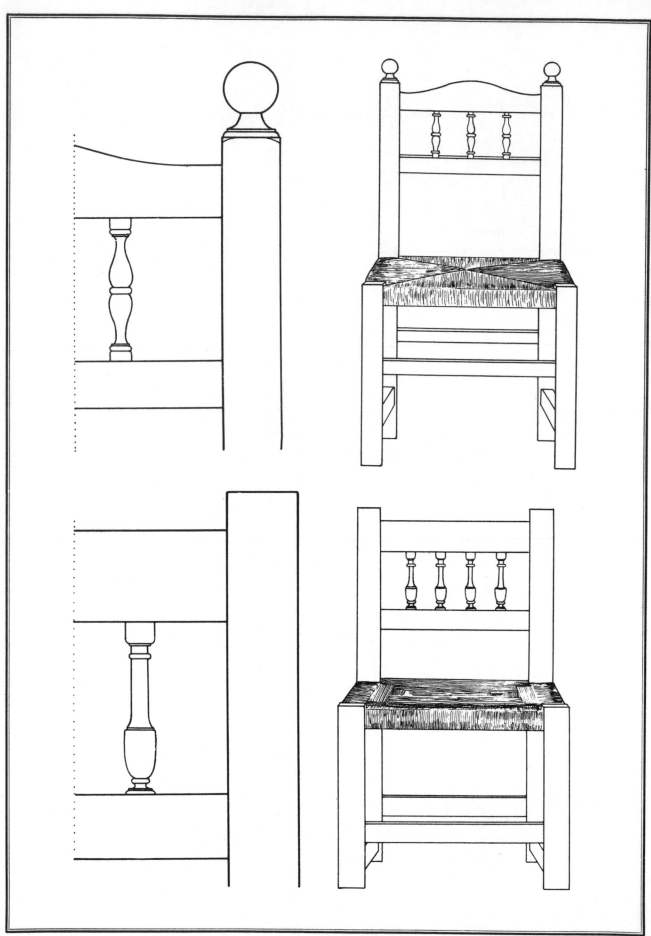

PLATE 220
Two chairs of folk design.

Hostería del Estudiante, Alcalá de Henares

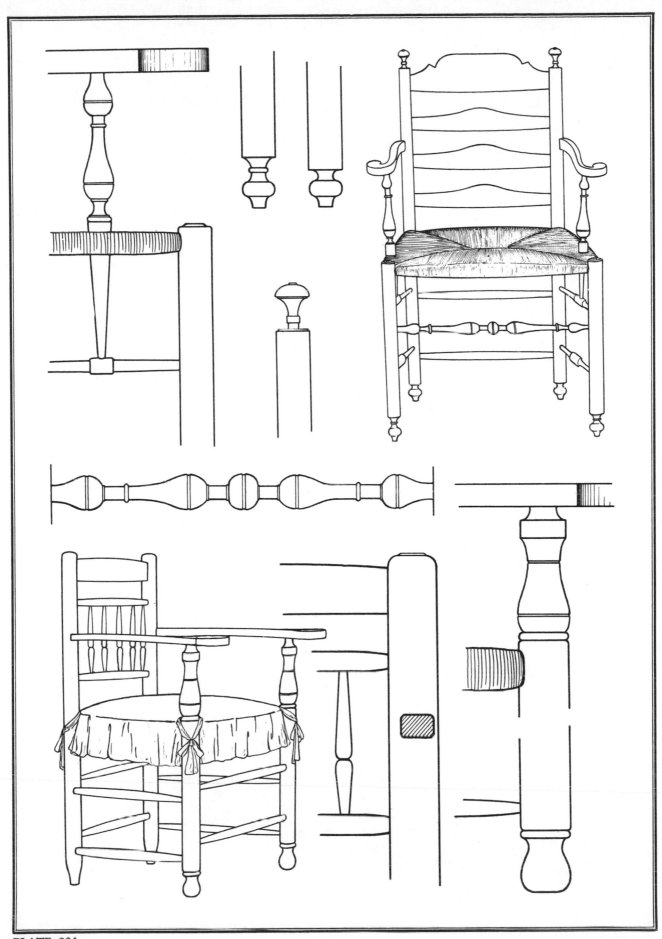

PLATE 221
Two armchairs of folk design.

Laguardia, Alava and Manor house in Santander

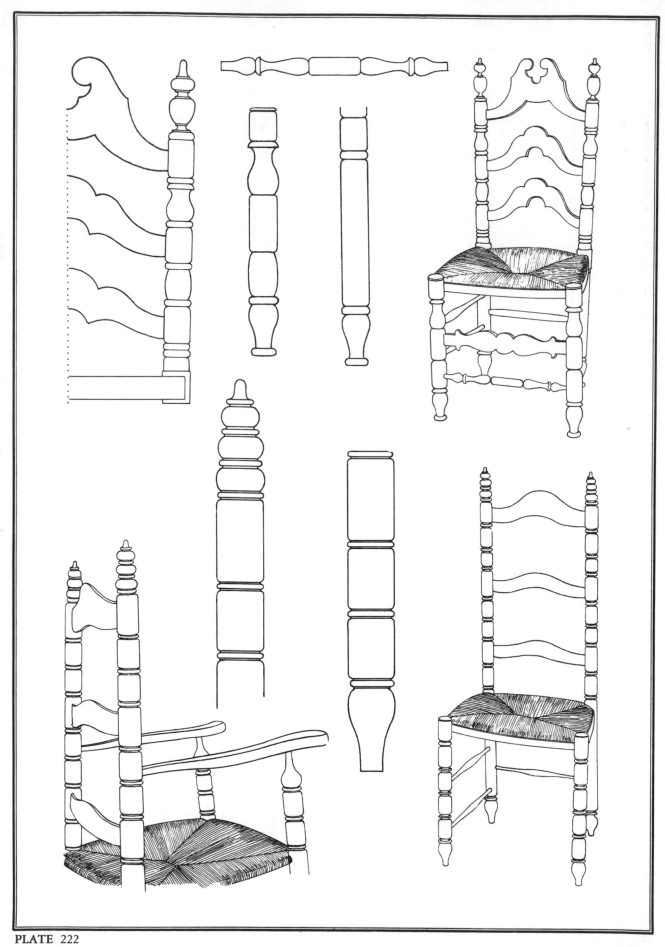

PLATE 222
Two chairs of folk design.

Archeological Museum of Seville and Manor house in Santander

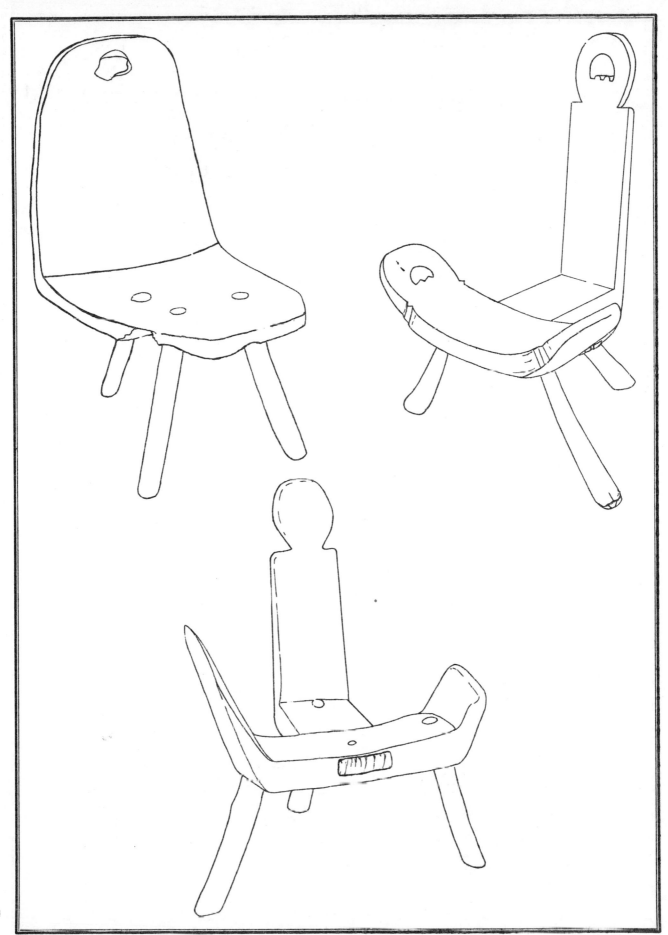

PLATE 223
Rustic three-legged chairs.

PLATE 224
Folk-style table.

Museum of Decorative Arts, Madrid

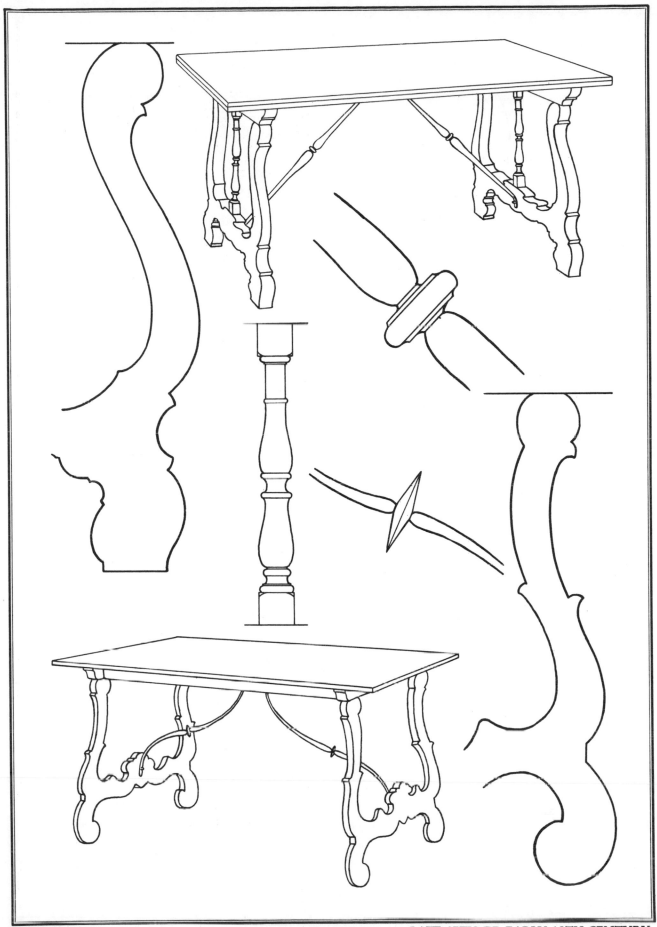

PLATE 225

LATE 17TH OR EARLY 18TH CENTURY

Tables with legs cut from wood and with wrought-iron ligatures.

Parador of Gredos, Avila and Parador of Ubeda, Jaen.

PLATE 226
Tables with legs cut from wood and with wrought-iron ligatures.

LATE 17TH OR EARLY 18TH CENTURY

Quinta de Raixa, Palma de Mallorca

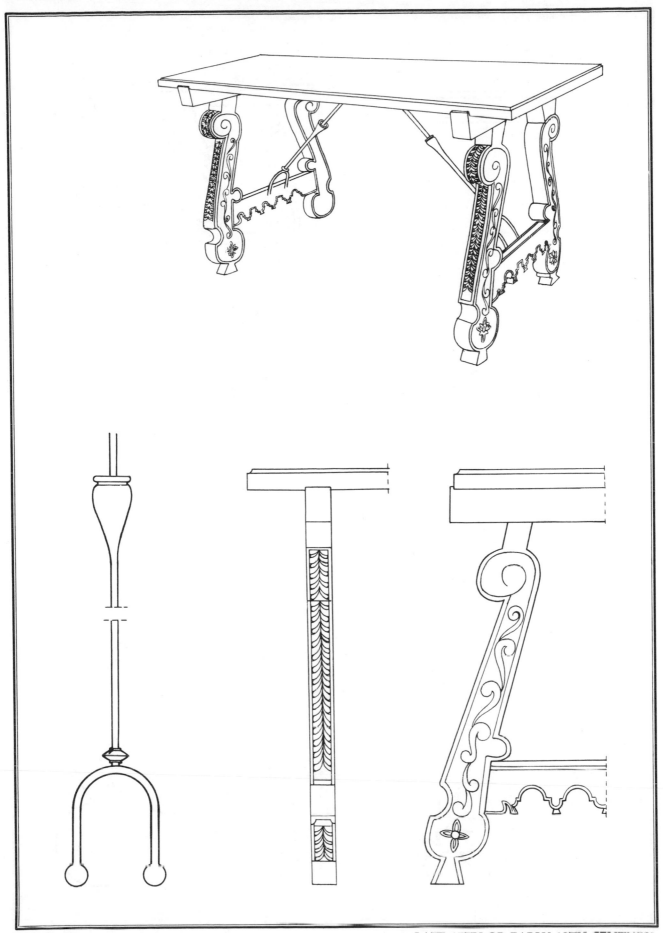

PLATE 227
Table with cut and carved wooden legs and wrought-iron ligatures.

LATE 17TH OR EARLY 18TH CENTURY

Museum of Decorative Arts, Madrid

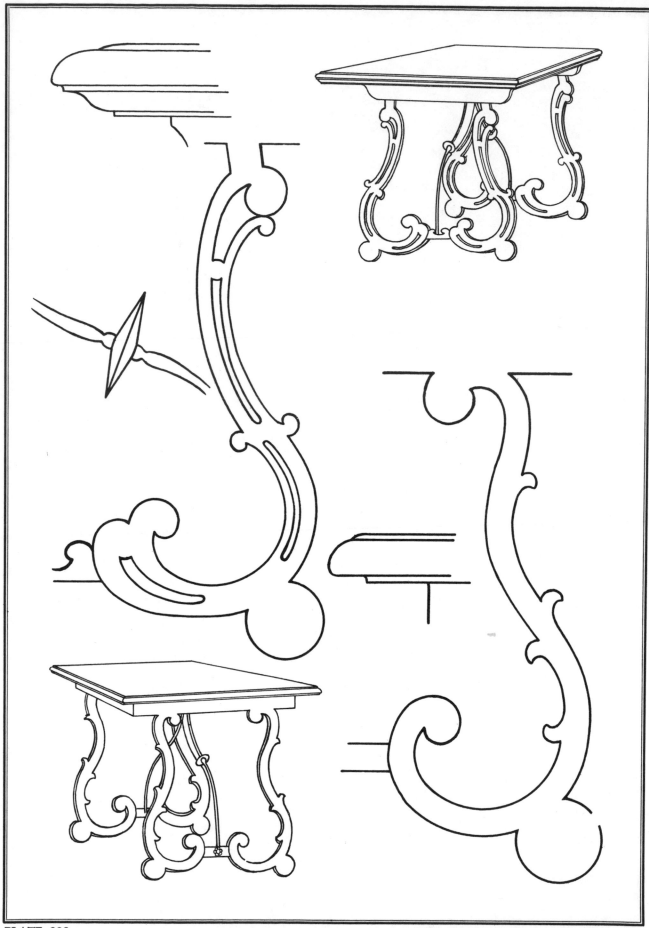

PLATE 228
Small tables with cut wooden legs and wrought-iron ligatures.

LATE 17TH OR EARLY 18TH CENTURY

Weisberger collection, Madrid

PLATE 229
Chair and armchair with "bridge" backs and turned wooden legs.

LATE 17TH OR EARLY 18TH CENTURY

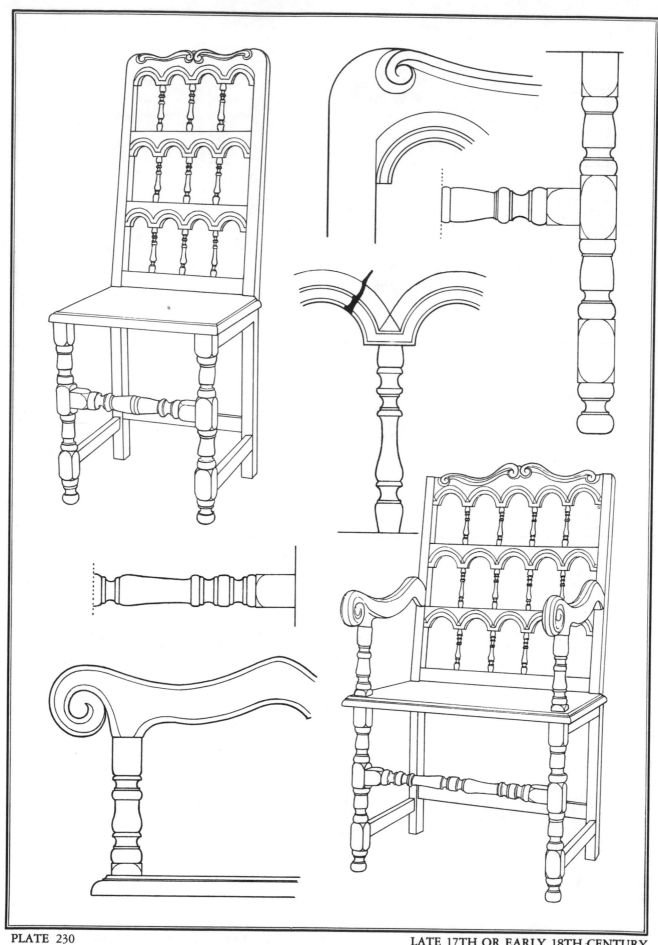

PLATE 230
Chair and armchair with "bridge" backs and turned legs.

LATE 17TH OR EARLY 18TH CENTURY

From a manor house in Huesca province

PLATE 231

Brazier supported by balusters and decorated with engraved vegetable motifs.

Marqués de la Cenia collection, Palma de Mallorca

PLATE 232   LATE 17TH OR EARLY 18TH CENTURY
Bench with wrought-iron hinges and crosspieces and cut legs. Marquetry decoration.

Valencia Don Juan Institute, Madrid

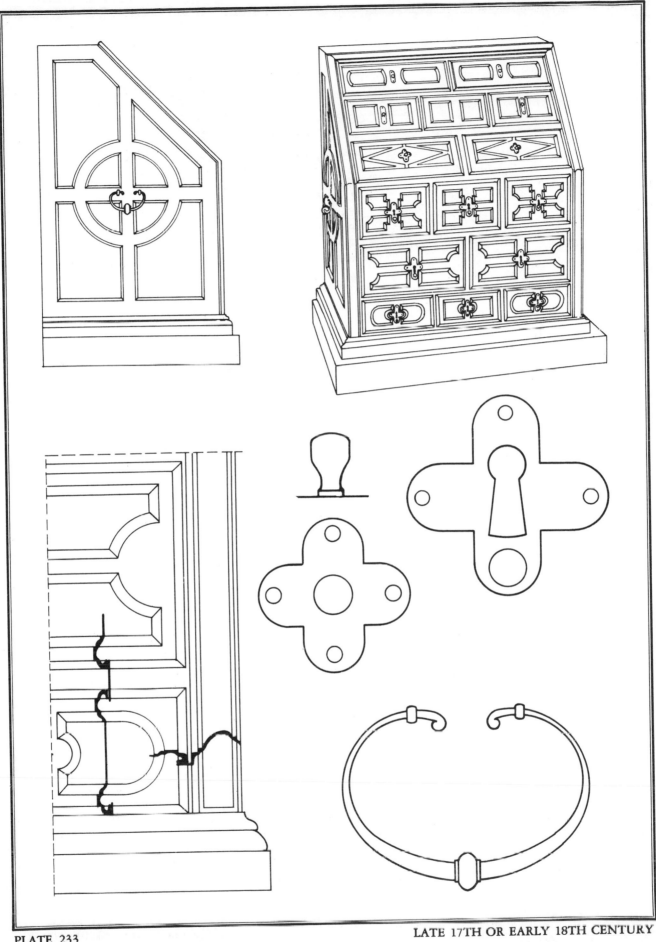

PLATE 233
Commode decorated with mouldings.

LATE 17TH OR EARLY 18TH CENTURY

Museum of Decorative Arts, Madrid

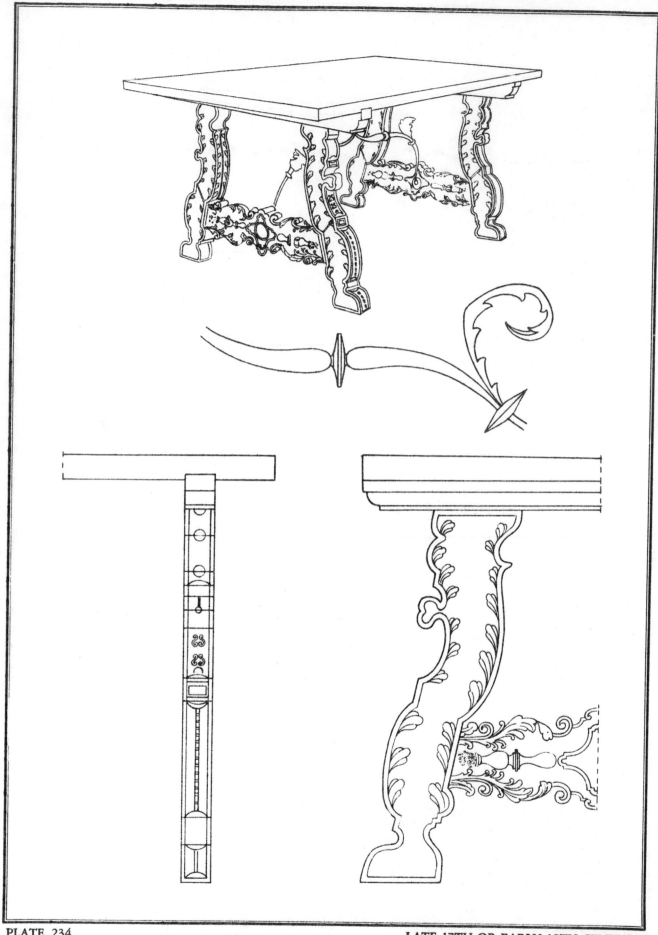

PLATE 234   LATE 17TH OR EARLY 18TH CENTURY
Carved table with legs of cut wood and with wrought-iron "bobèche" crosspieces.

Museum of Decorative Arts, Madrid

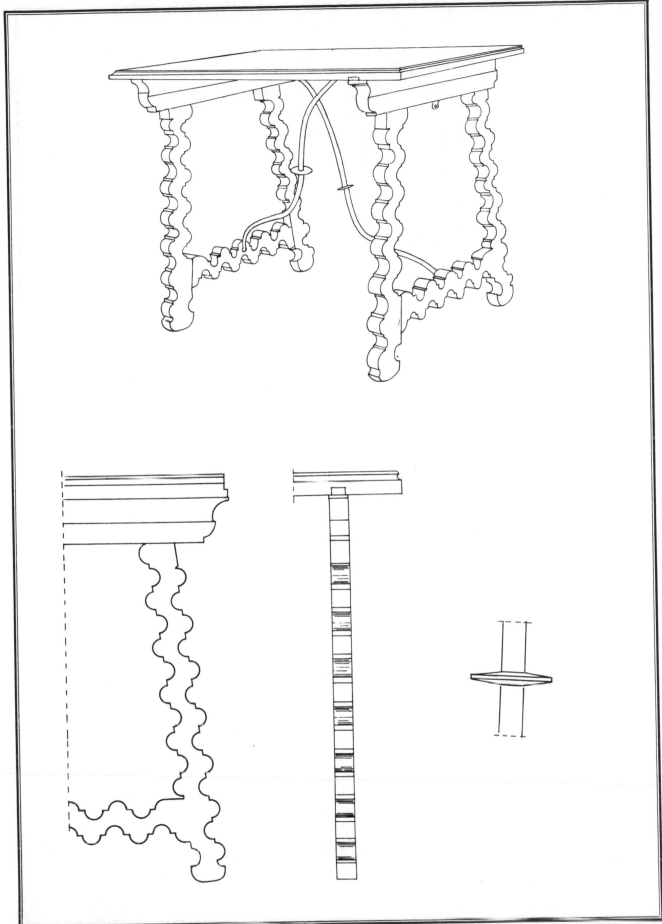

PLATE 235

LATE 17TH OR EARLY 18TH CENTURY

Table with wooden legs cut in a wavy pattern and with wrought-iron crosspieces.

Romantic Museum and Fundaciones Vega Inclán, Madrid

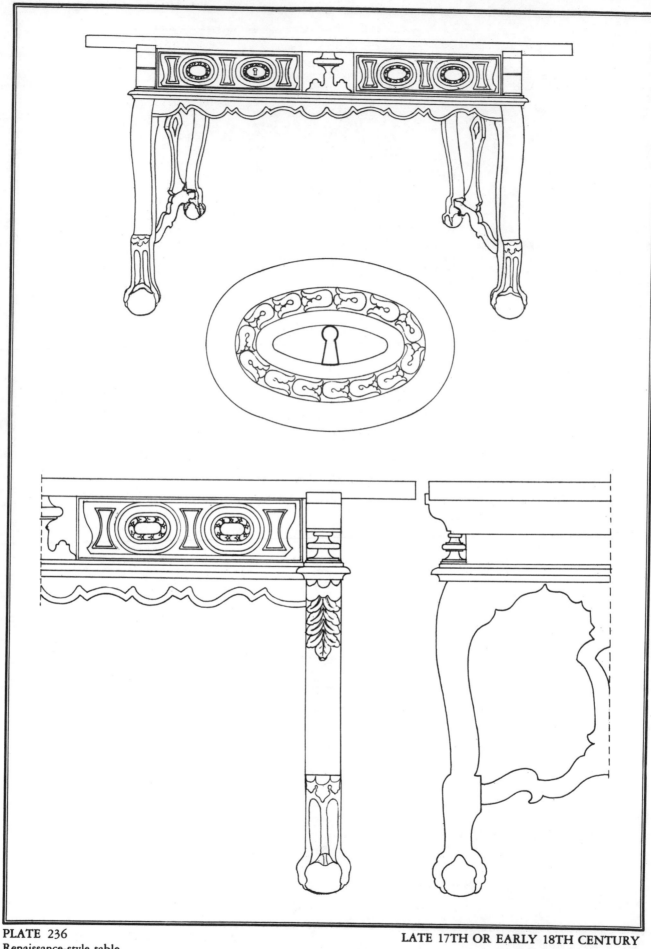

PLATE 236
Renaissance-style table.

LATE 17TH OR EARLY 18TH CENTURY

Museum of Decorative Arts, Madrid

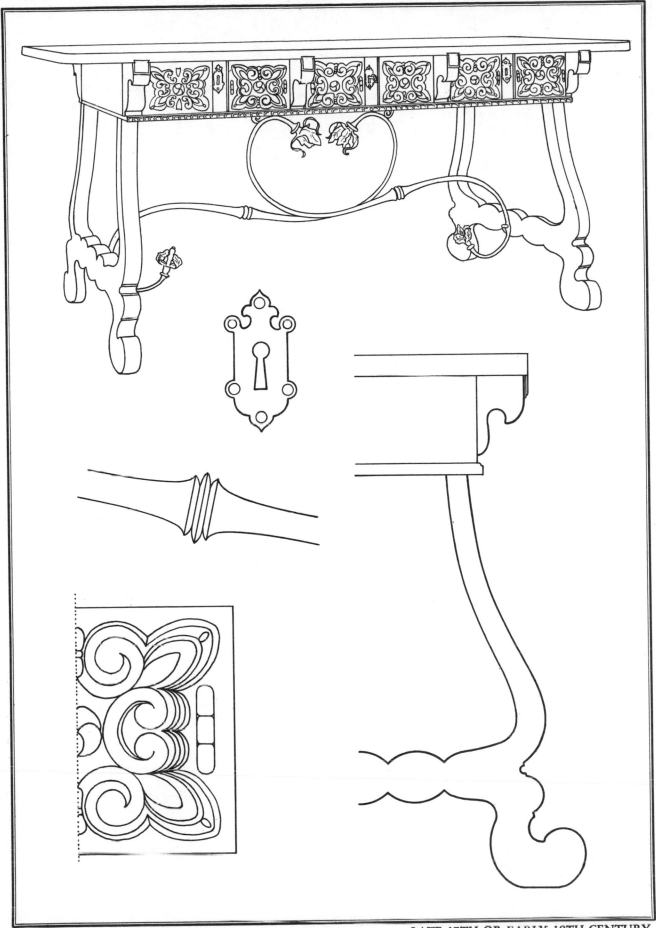

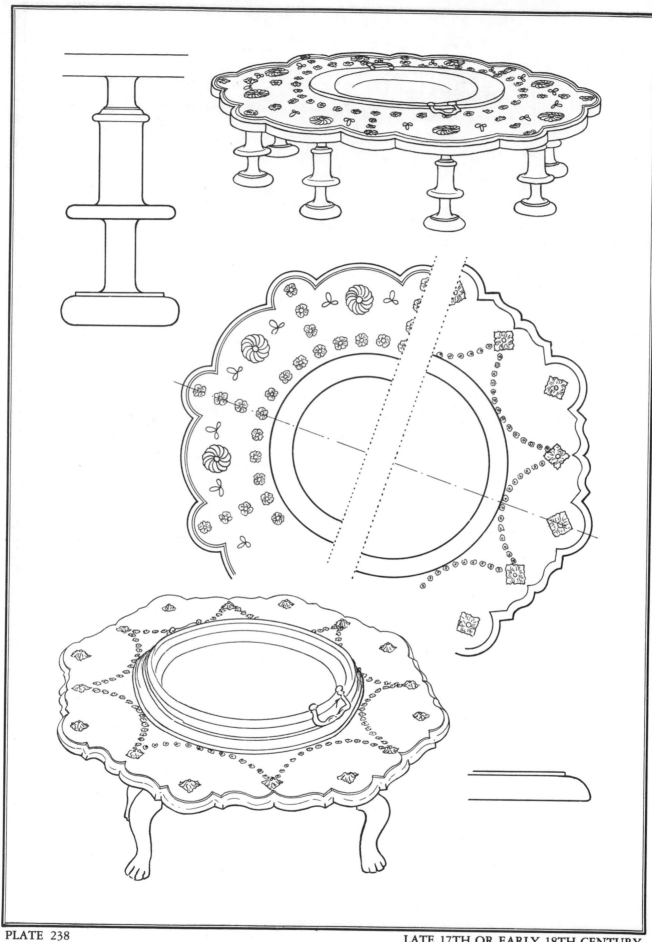

PLATE 238
Braziers.

PLATE 239
Four lanterns of folk design.

Parador of Toledo and Inns in Alcalá de Henares and Gredos

PLATE 240
Chest of folk design.

LATE 17TH OR EARLY 18TH CENTURY

Museum of Decorative Arts, Madrid

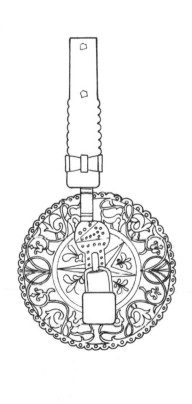

PLATE 241
Chest.

LATE 17TH OR EARLY 18TH CENTURY

Museum of Decorative Arts, Madrid

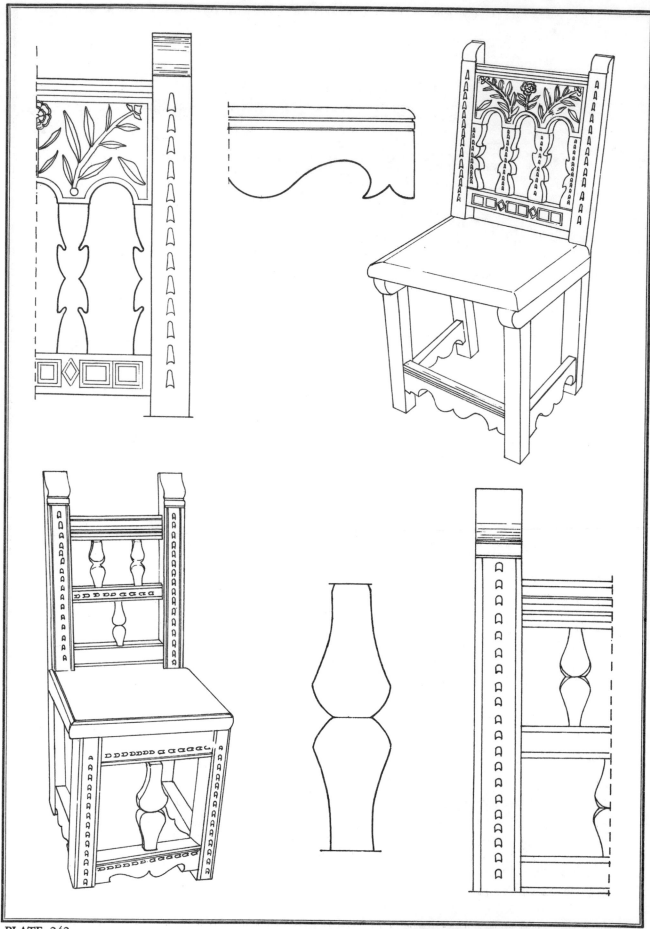

PLATE 242
Chairs of folk design.

LATE 17TH OR EARLY 18TH CENTURY

Museum of Decorative Arts, Madrid

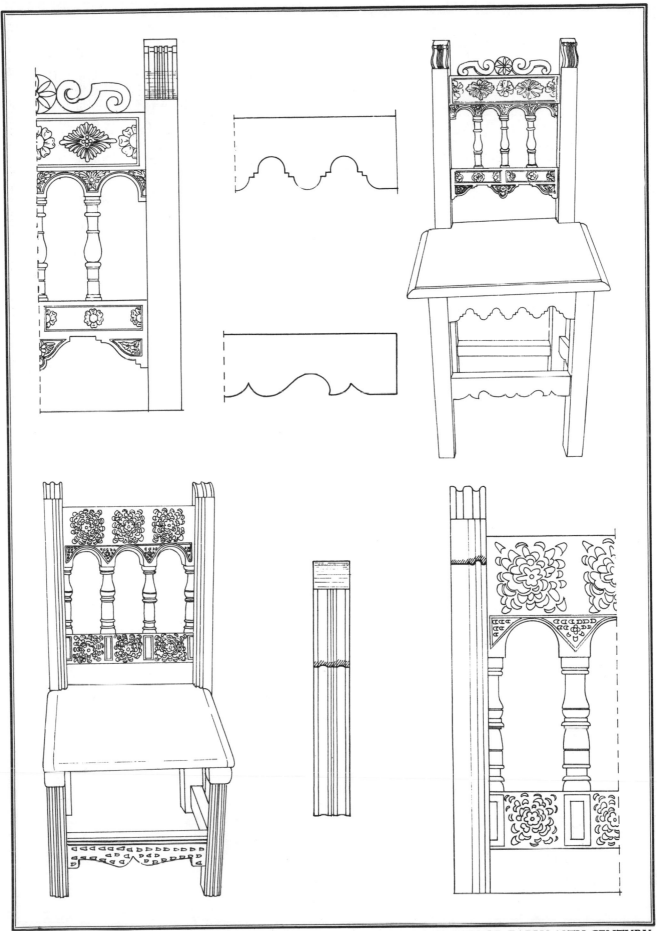

PLATE 243
Chairs of folk design.

Museum of Decorative Arts, Madrid

PLATE 244
Chairs of folk design.

Museum of Decorative Arts, Madrid

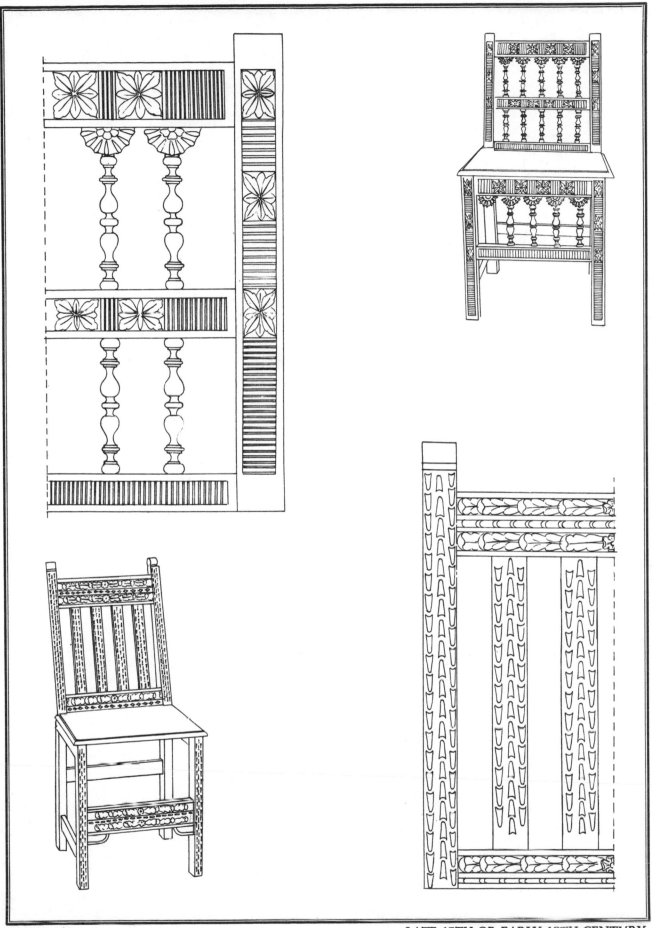

PLATE 245
Chairs of folk design.

LATE 17TH OR EARLY 18TH CENTURY

Upper chair: Museum of Decorative Arts, Madrid

PLATE 246
Chairs of folk design.

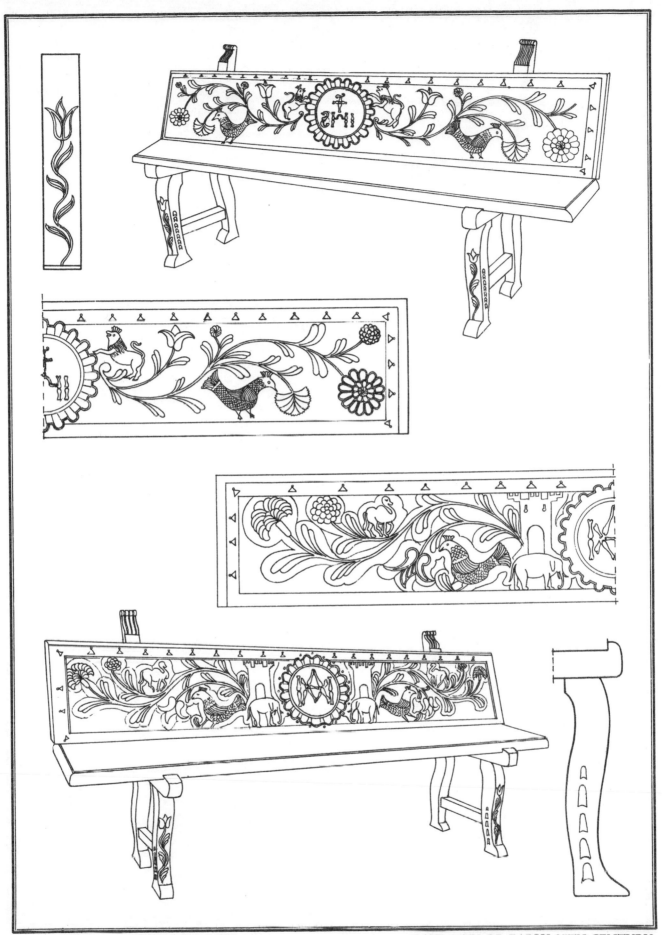

PLATE 247
Folk-style benches with decorative carvings.

LATE 17TH OR EARLY 18TH CENTURY

Museum of Decorative Arts and Romantic Museum, Madrid

PLATE 248
Buffet of folk design.

LATE 17TH OR EARLY 18TH CENTURY

Tavera Hospital, Toledo

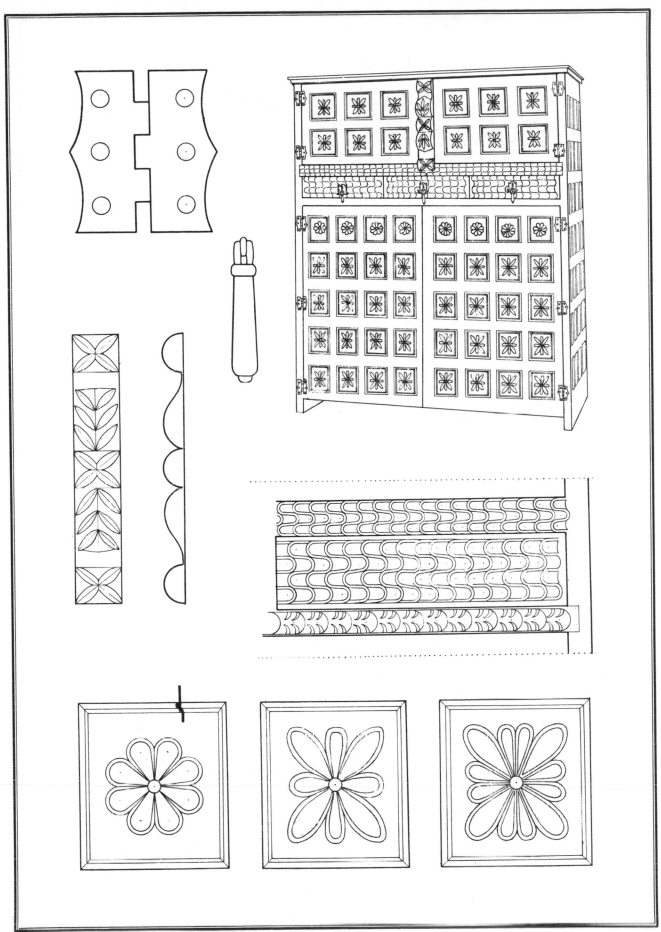

PLATE 249
Wardrobe of folk design in two pieces.

Tavera Hospital, Toledo

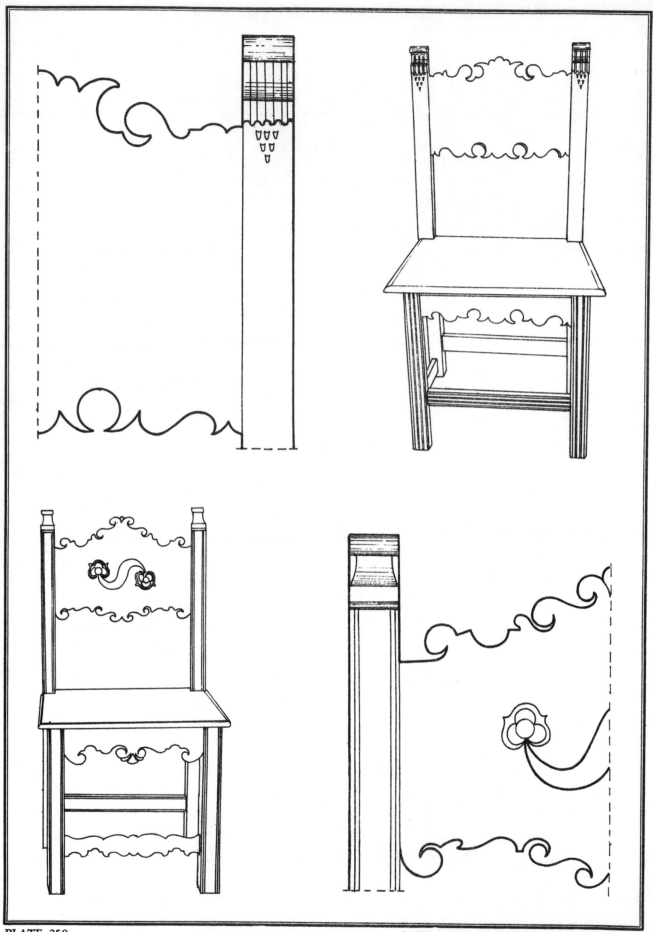

PLATE 250
Two chairs of folk design.

LATE 17TH OR EARLY 18TH CENTURY

Museum of Decorative Arts, Madrid

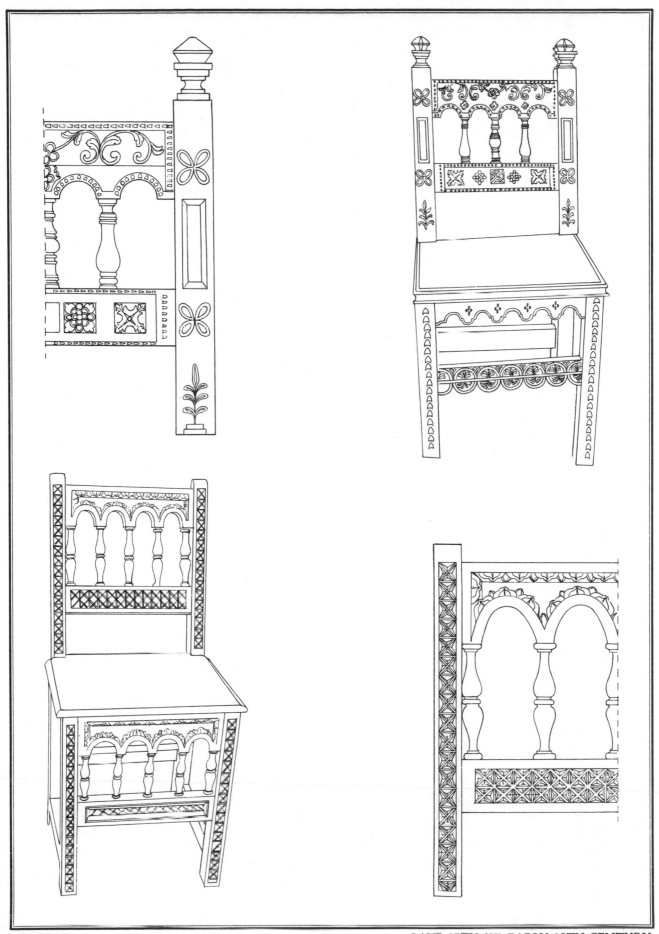

PLATE 251
Chairs of folk design.

LATE 17TH OR EARLY 18TH CENTURY

National Archeological Museum and Museum of Decorative Arts, Madrid

PLATE 252
Chairs of folk design.

PLATE 253
Chairs of folk design.

LATE 17TH OR EARLY 18TH CENTURY

Gustavo Gili collection, Santillana del Mar

PLATE 254
Chair and armchair of folk design.

Beancharro collection, Pontevedra

PLATE 255
Folk-style armchairs.

Museum of Decorative Arts, Madrid

PLATE 256
Folk-style chairs.

18TH CENTURY

Museum of Decorative Arts, Madrid

PLATE 257
Folk-style chairs.

Parador of Gredos, Avila

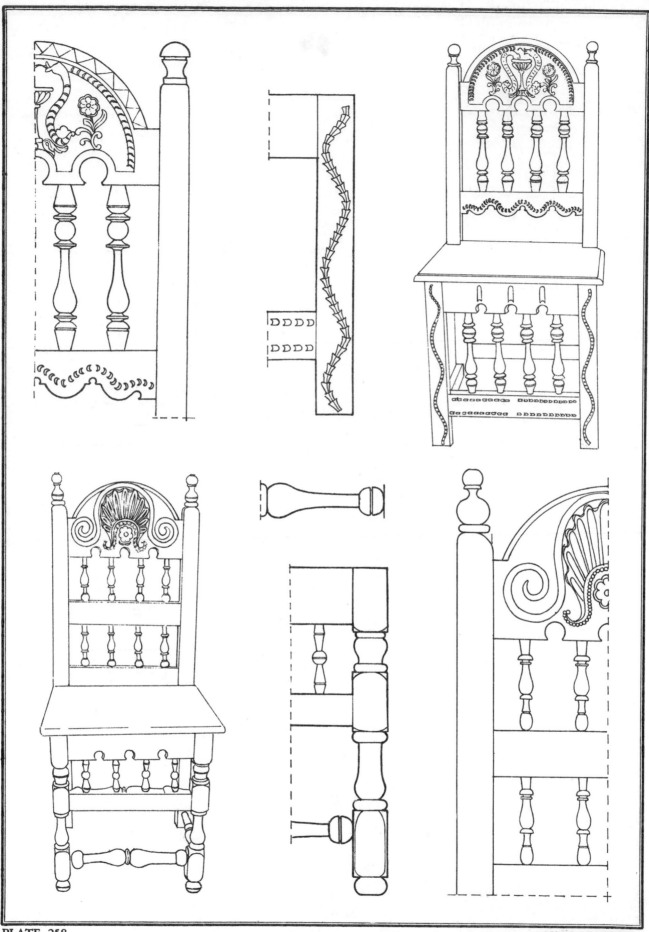

PLATE 258
Folk-style chairs.

Museum of Decorative Arts, Madrid

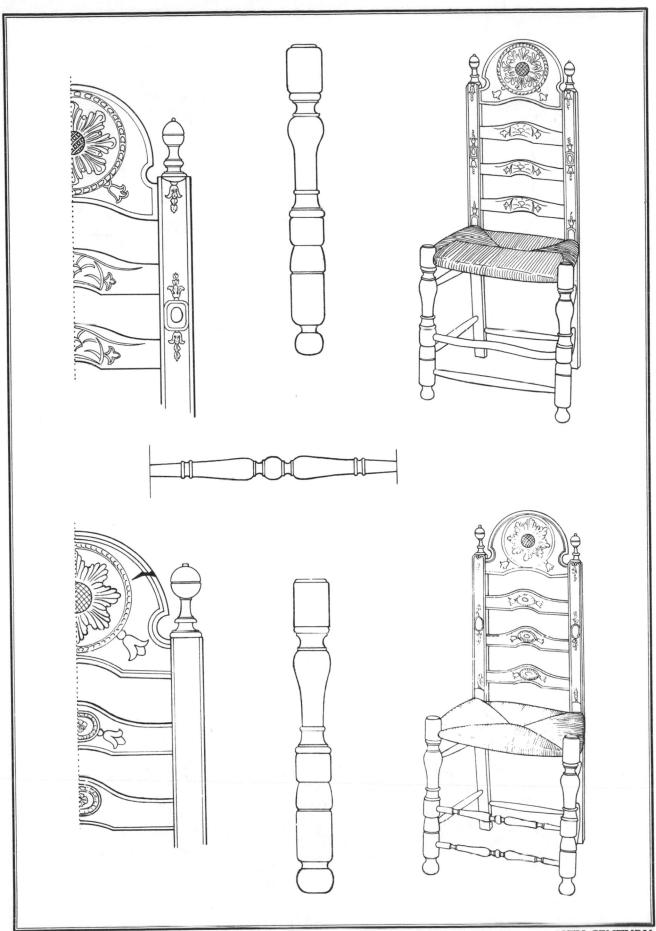

PLATE 259
Chairs.

Museum of Decorative Arts, Madrid

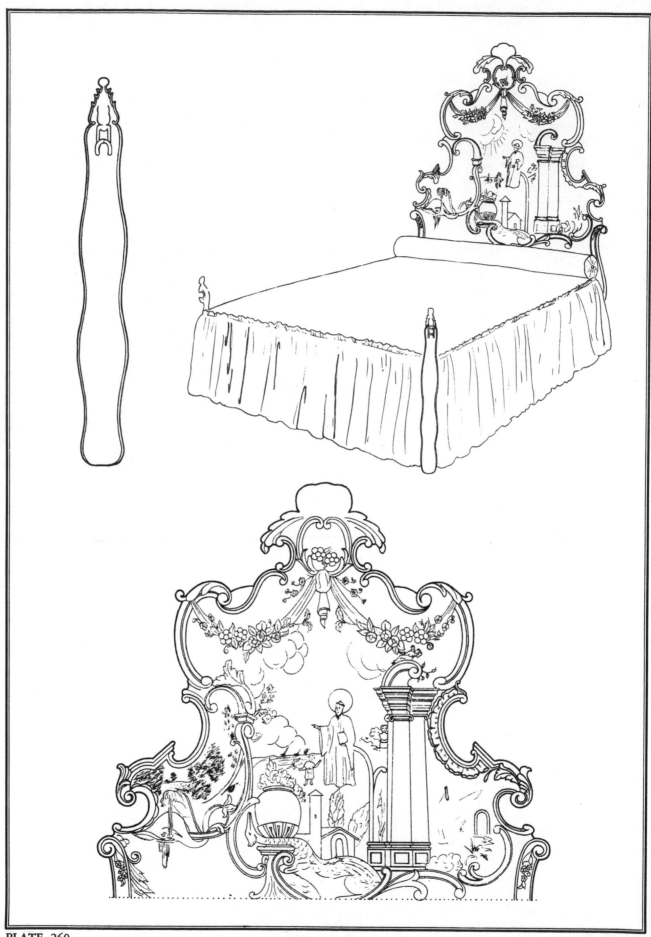

PLATE 260
Catalonian bed with painted headboard.

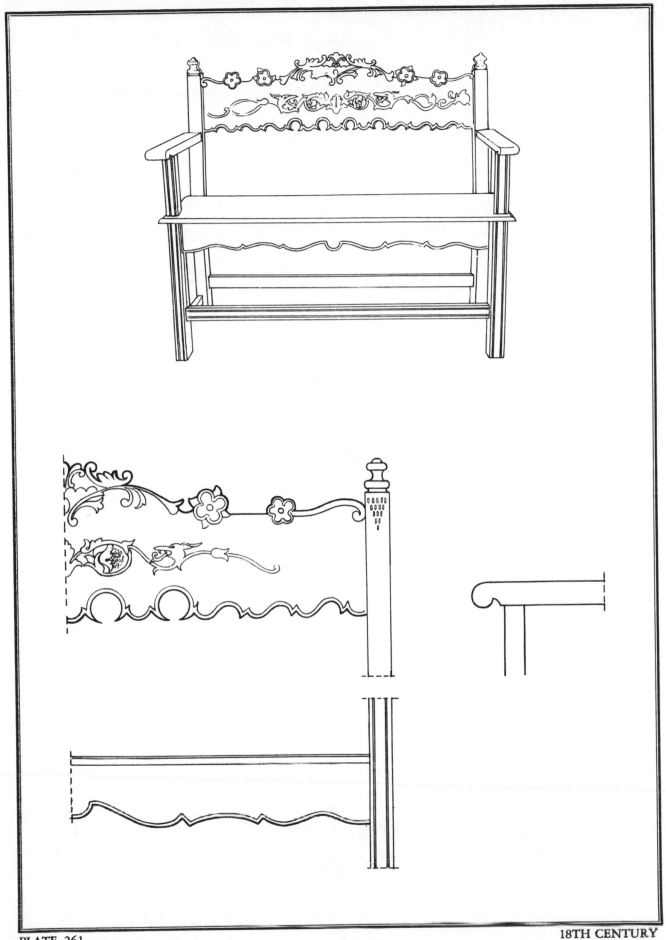

PLATE 261
Folk-style bench with carved back.

18TH CENTURY

Romantic Museum, Madrid

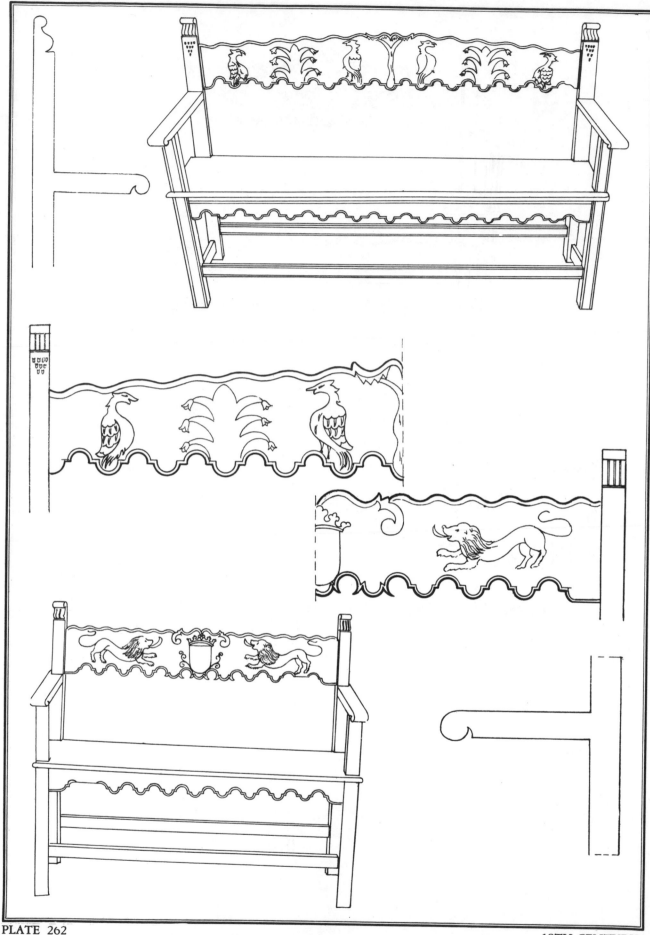

PLATE 262
Folk-style benches with carved backs.

Romantic Museum, Madrid

PLATE 263
Two sofas of baroque design.

Parador of San Francisco, Granada and Museum of Painting, Seville

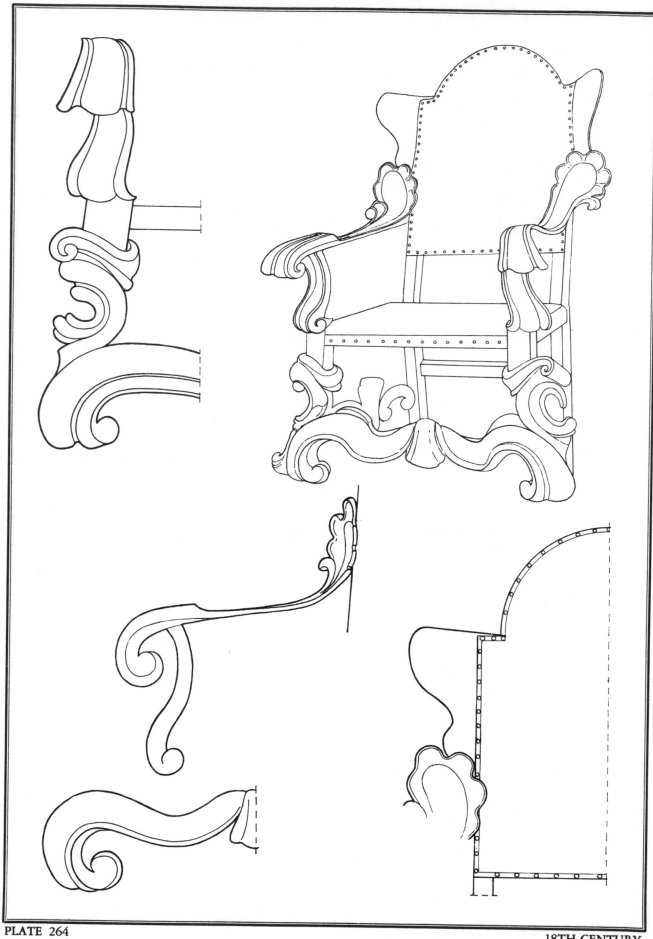

PLATE 264
Baroque armchair of Padre Alvarez de Sotomayor.

Private collection

PLATE 265
Folk-style bench.

Municipal Museum, Madrid

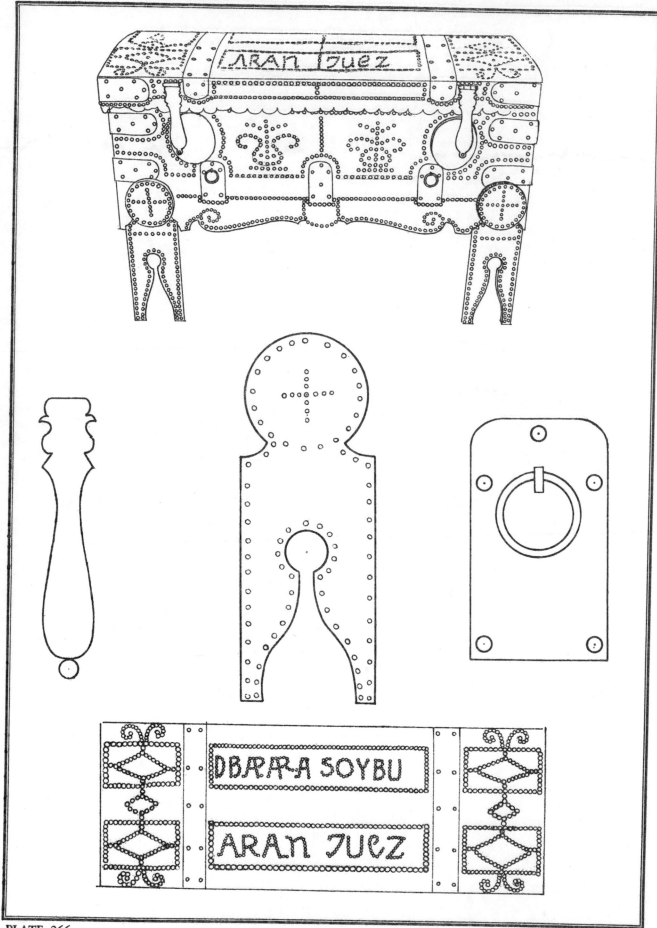

PLATE 266
Large leather chest with decorative nails.

18TH CENTURY

Museum of Decorative Arts, Madrid

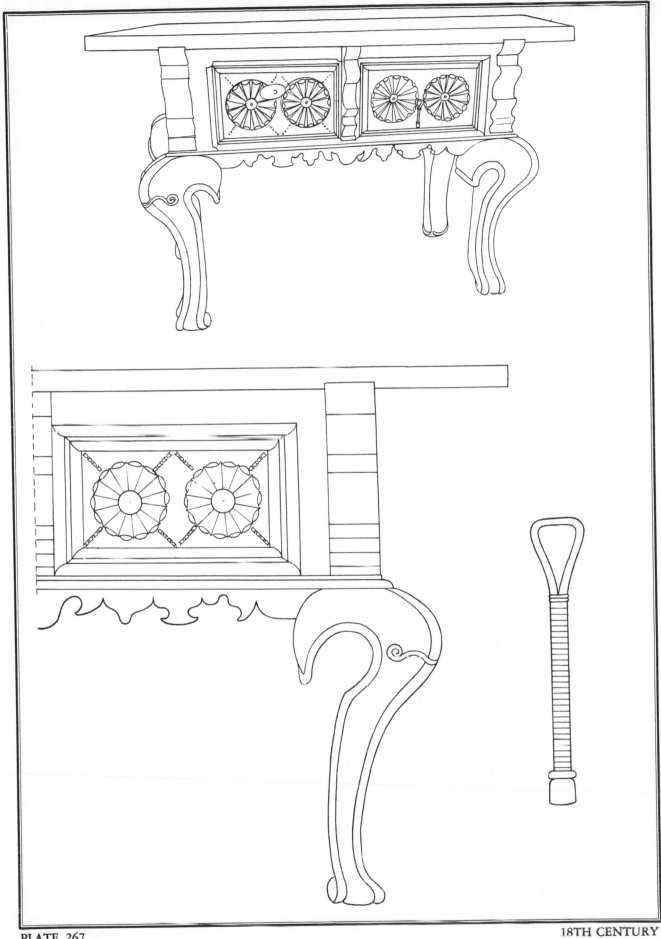

PLATE 267
Folk-style table.

Museum of Decorative Arts, Madrid

PLATE 268
Catalonian bed with painted headboard.

PLATE 269
Catalonian baroque-style bed.

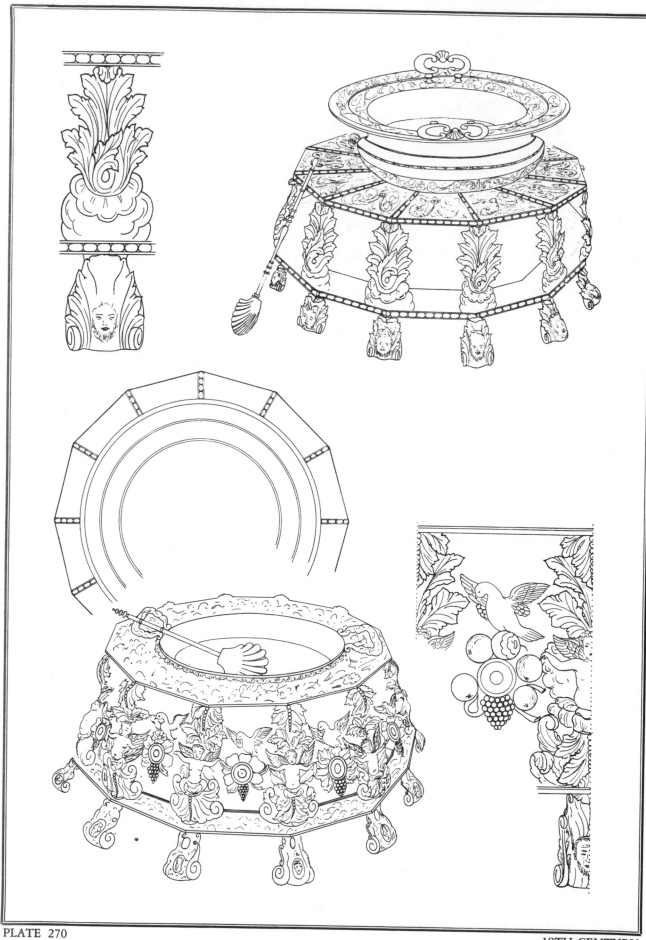

PLATE 270
Braziers.

18TH CENTURY

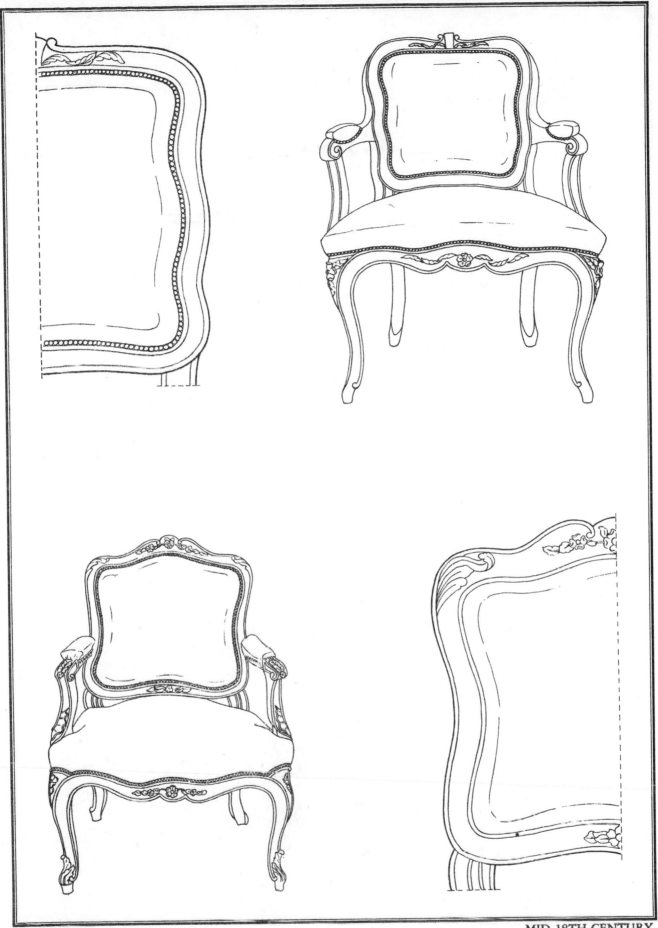

PLATE 271
Louis XV armchairs.

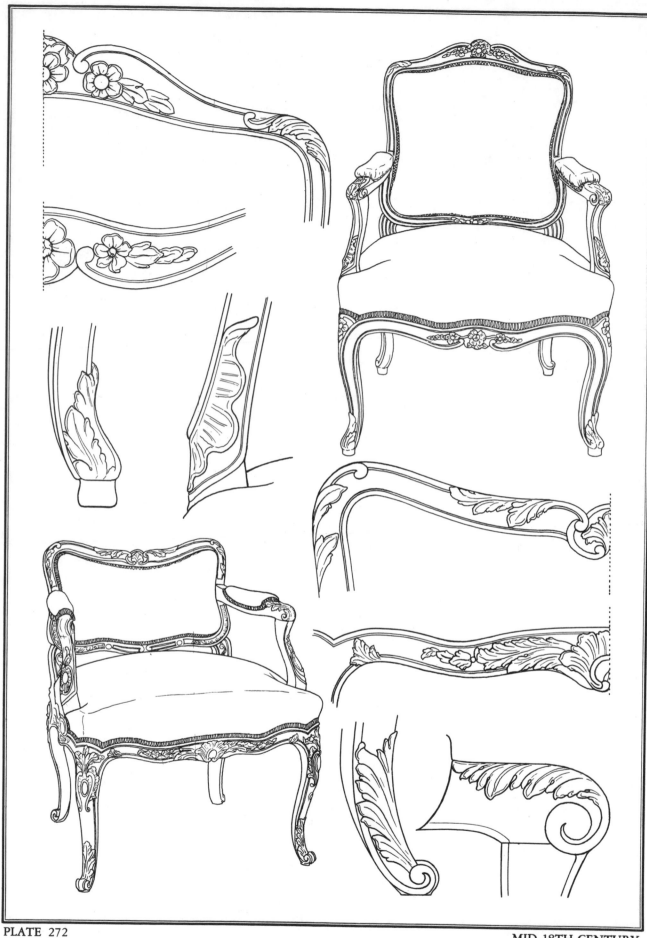

PLATE 272
Louis XV armchairs.

Royal Palace, Madrid

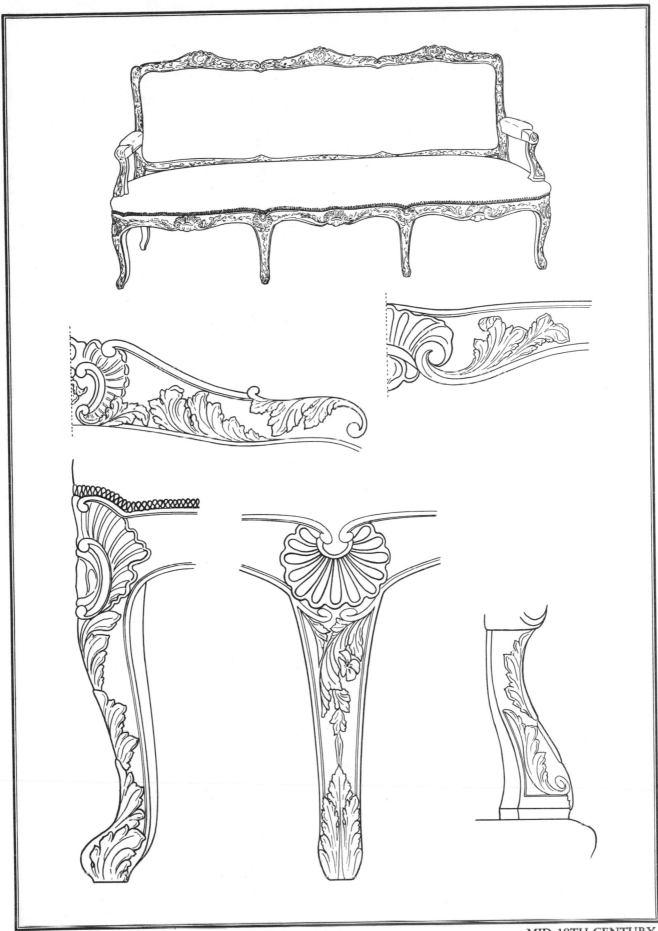

PLATE 273
Louis XV sofa.

MID-18TH CENTURY

Royal Palace, Madrid

277

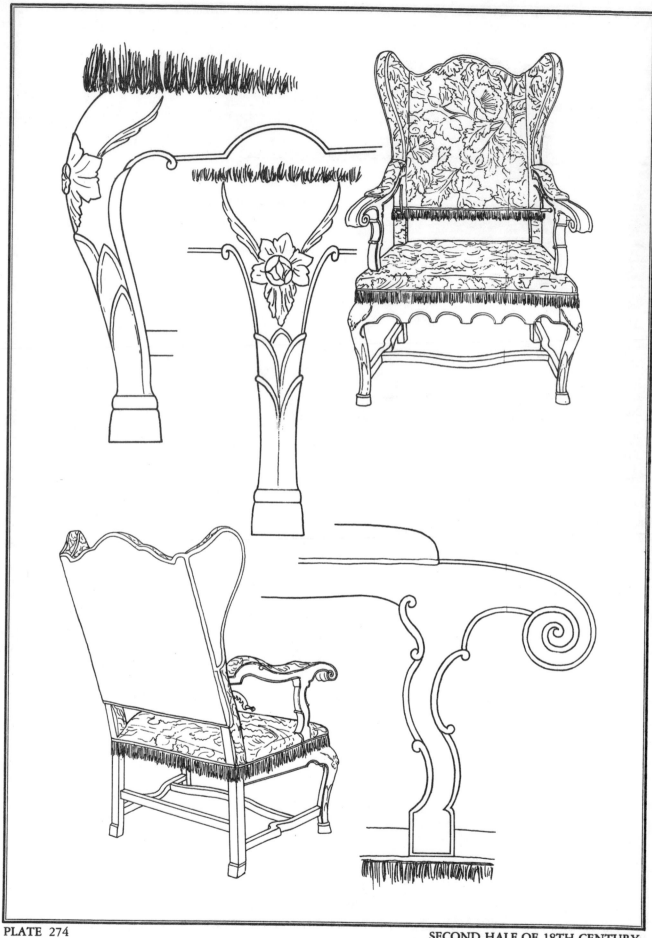

PLATE 274
Winged armchair, "Voltaire" style.

PLATE 275

Baroque armchair and footstool, to hold a statue of the Virgin Mary. Louis XV armchair.

Museum of Decorative Arts, Madrid

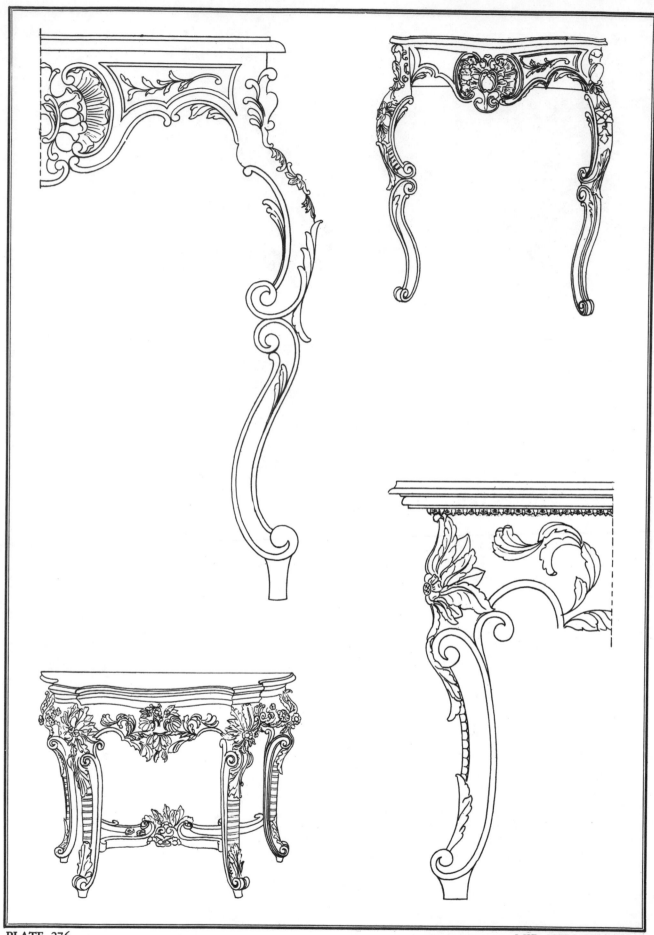

PLATE 277
Baroque consoles inspired by the lines of the Louis XV style.

SECOND THIRD OF 18TH CENTURY

Municipal Museum, Madrid

PLATE 278
Baroque consoles, along the lines of the Louis XV style.

SECOND THIRD OF 18TH CENTURY

Municipal Museum, Madrid

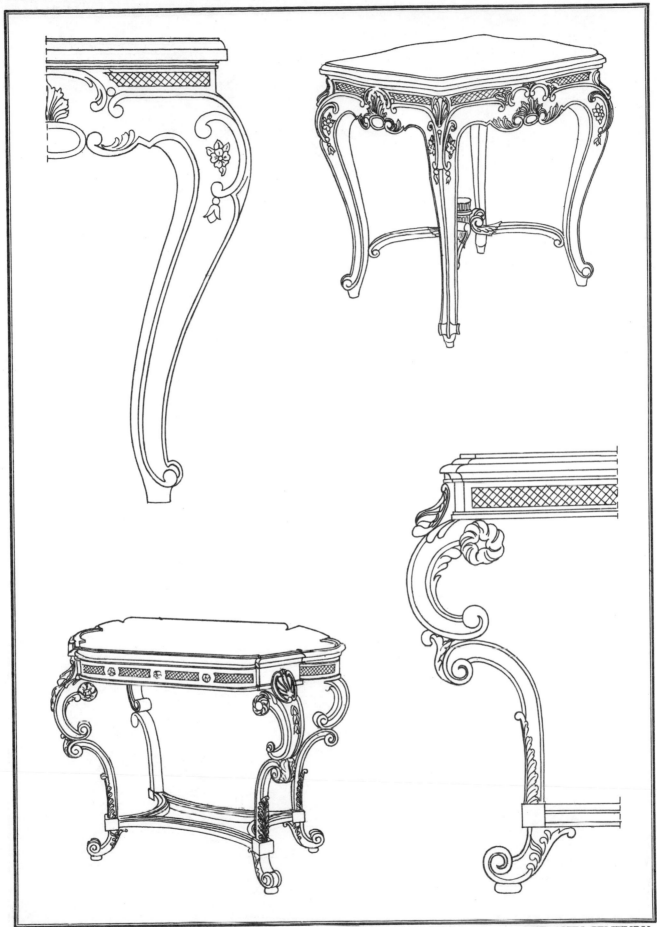

PLATE 279
Louis XV console tables.

Municipal Museum, Madrid

PLATE 280
Small console, shelf and canopy decorated with baroque carvings.

SECOND HALF OF 18TH CENTURY

PLATE 281
Small console and mirror decorated with baroque carvings.

SECOND HALF OF 18TH CENTURY

PLATE 282
Mirror framed with Central European style of baroque carvings.

FIRST HALF OF 18TH CENTURY

Museum of Painting, Seville

PLATE 283
Frame decorated with Central European style of baroque carvings.

FIRST HALF OF 18TH CENTURY

Museum of Decorative Arts, Madrid

287

PLATE 284
Frame decorated with Central European style of baroque carvings.

FIRST HALF OF 18TH CENTURY

Museum of Decorative Arts, Madrid

PLATE 285
Frame decorated with baroque carvings.

National Archeological Museum, Madrid

PLATE 286
Sconces with mirrors decorated with baroque carvings, inspired by the French "rococo."

Museum of Decorative Arts, Madrid

PLATE 287
Spanish sconce with mirror inspired by French "rococo."

Museum of Decorative Arts, Madrid

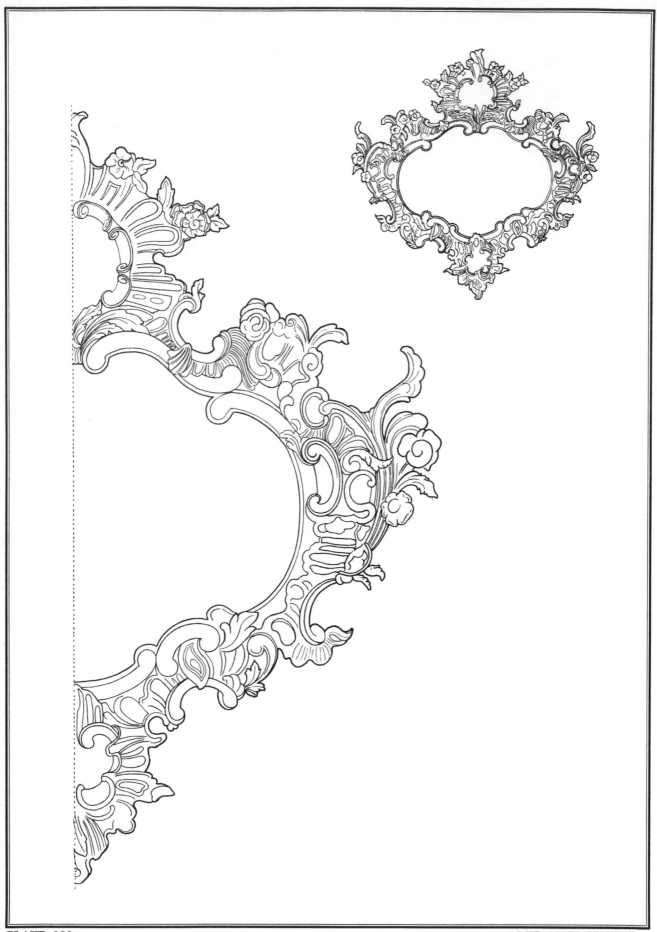

PLATE 288
Spanish sconce with mirror inspired by French "rococo."

Romantic Museum and Fundaciones Vega Inclán, Madrid

PLATE 289
Wardrobe decorated with baroque motifs.

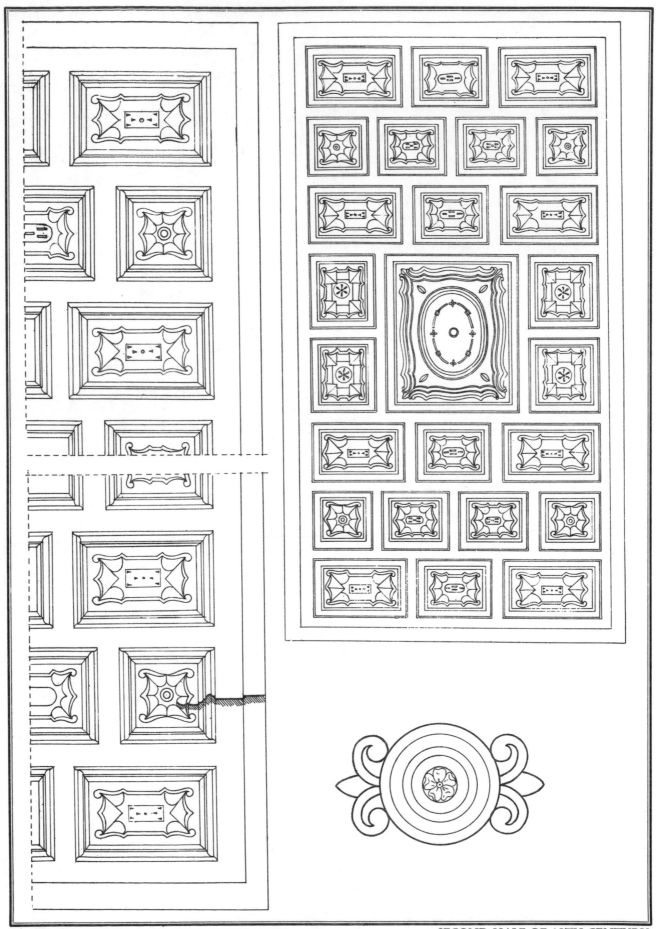

PLATE 290
Panelled door decorated with baroque motifs of Chinese origin.

SECOND HALF OF 18TH CENTURY

Private collection

PLATE 291
Door decorated with "rococo" carvings.

Museum of Decorative Arts, Madrid

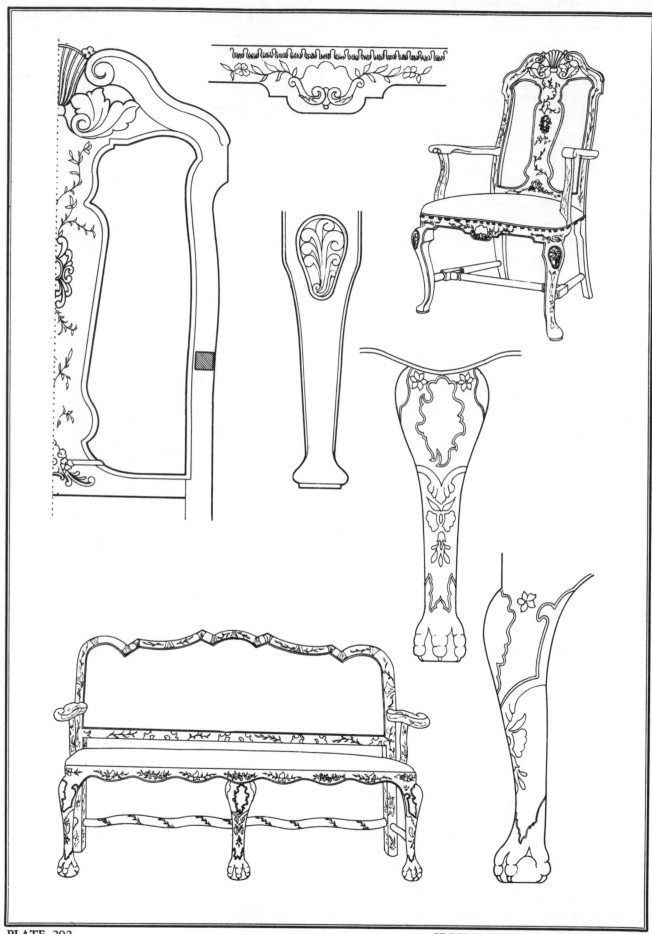

PLATE 292
Spanish armchair and sofa; inspired by the Queen Anne style.

SECOND HALF OF 18TH CENTURY

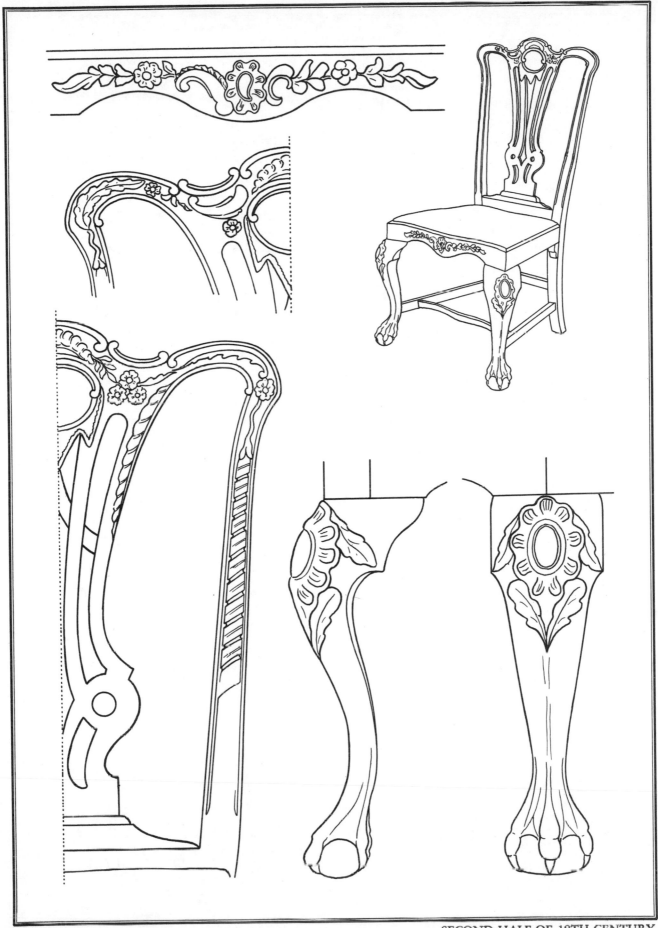

PLATE 293
Spanish chair inspired by the Queen Anne style.

SECOND HALF OF 18TH CENTURY

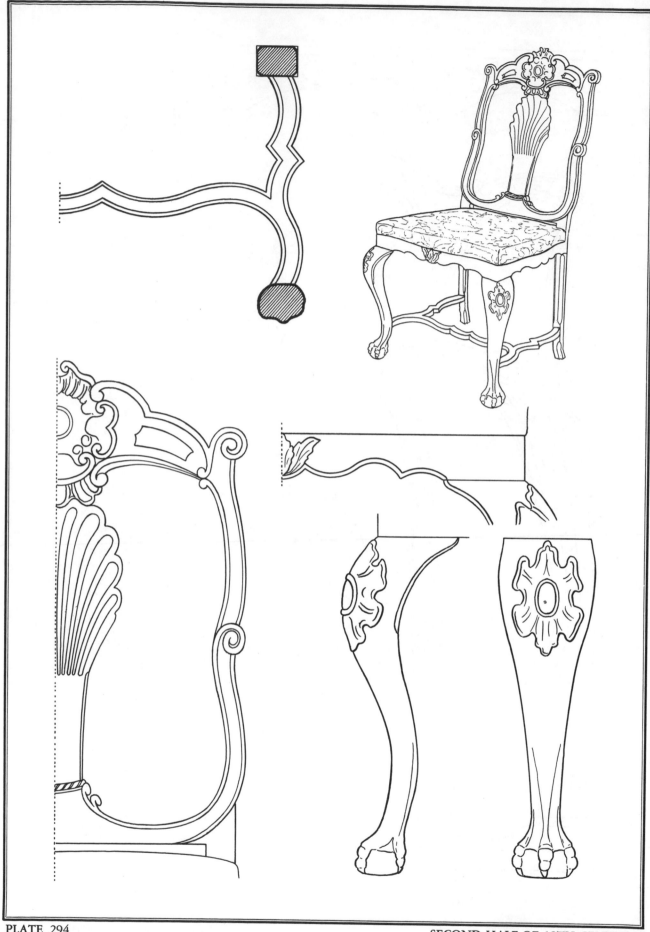

PLATE 294
Spanish Queen Anne chair.

PLATE 295
Chair decorated with baroque carvings, Spanish adaption of Queen Anne style.

National Archeological Museum, Madrid

PLATE 296
Console table supporting a miniature English-style commode-wardrobe.

SECOND HALF OF 18TH CENTURY

Valencia Don Juan Institute, Madrid

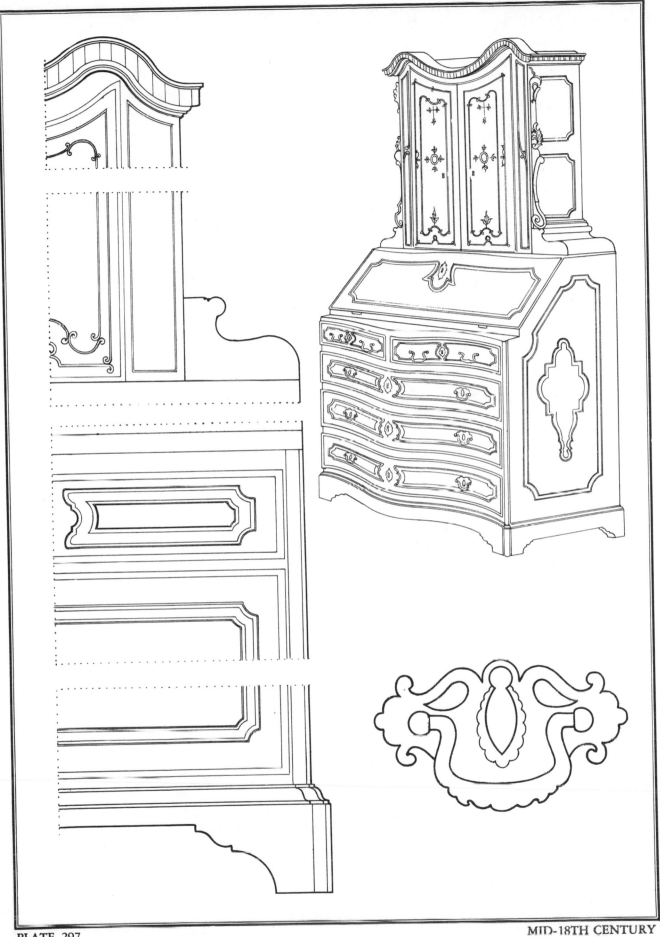

PLATE 297
English-style commode-wardrobe.

Municipal Museum, Madrid

PLATE 298
Small English-style console table. Mirror framed with baroque carving.

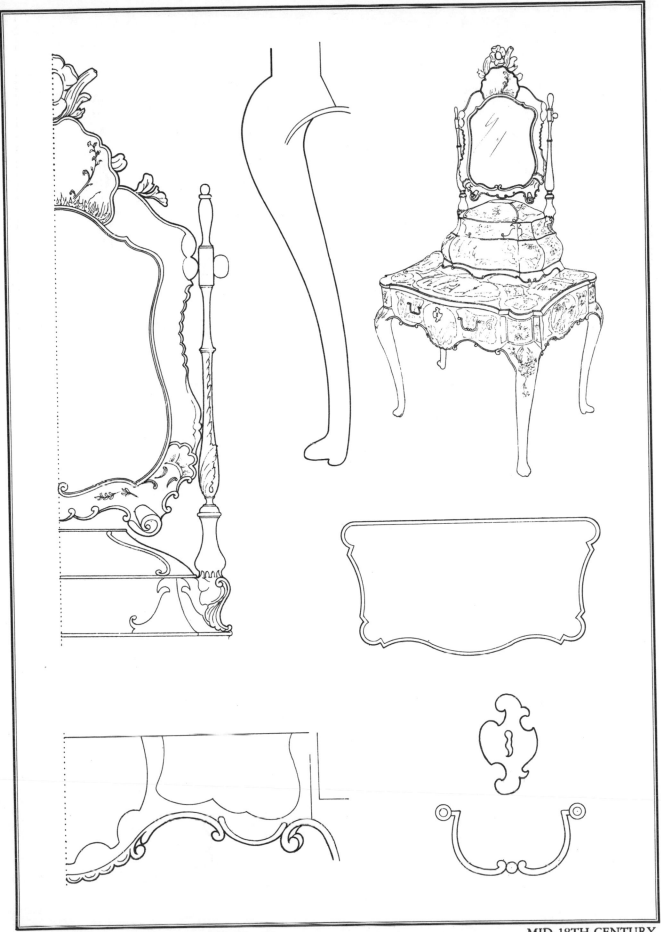

PLATE 299
Dressing table inspired by Queen Anne style.

MID-18TH CENTURY

Conde del Valle de Marles collection, Barcelona

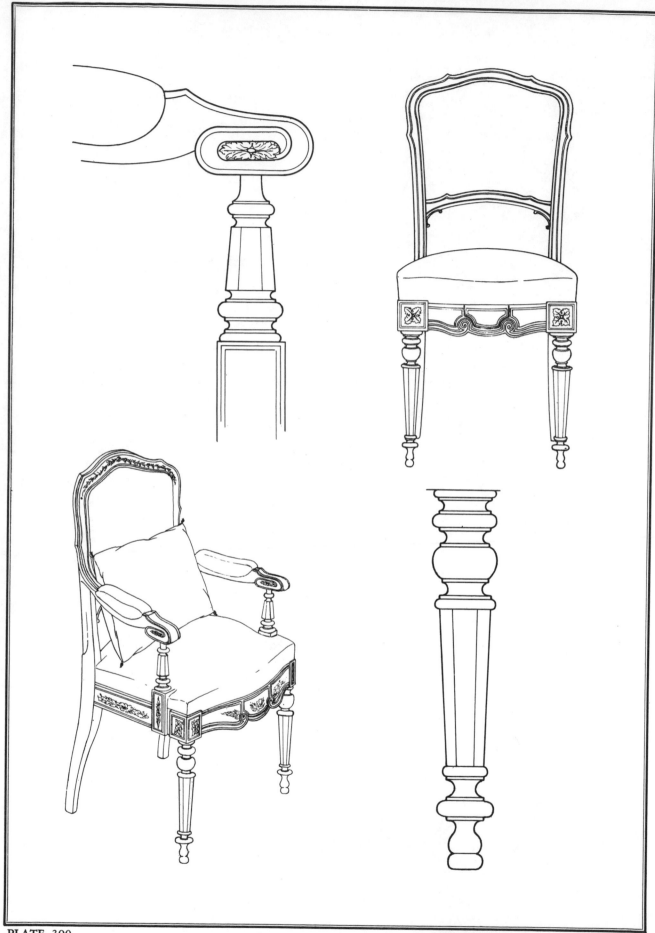

PLATE 300
Spanish chair and armchair inspired by Louis XVI style.

Palace of El Infante Don Alonso de Orleans, Sanlucar de Barrameda

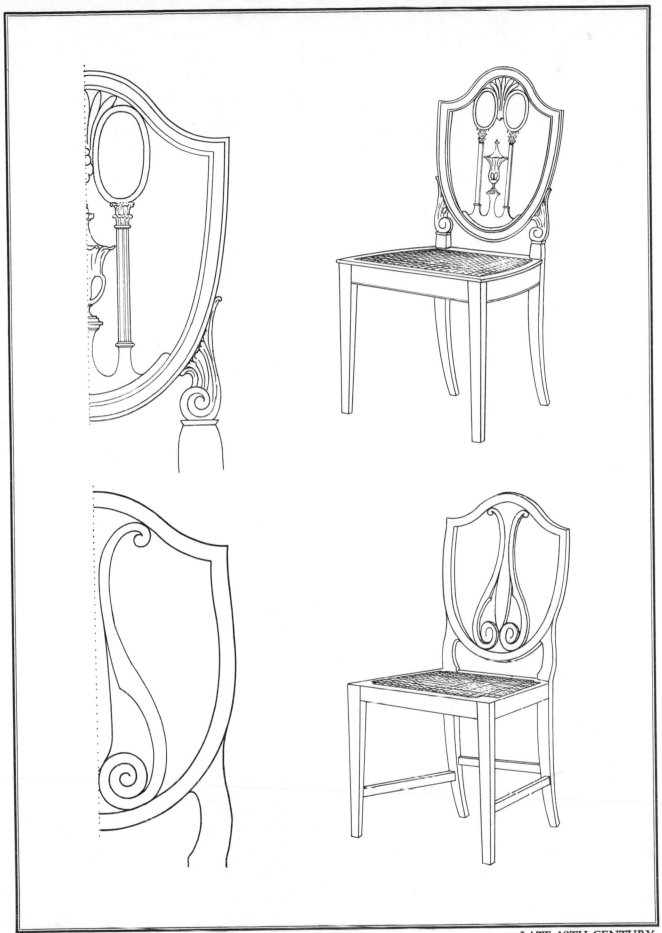

PLATE 301
Charles IV cane chairs.

Pontevedra Museum and Casa Cabanyes, Argentona

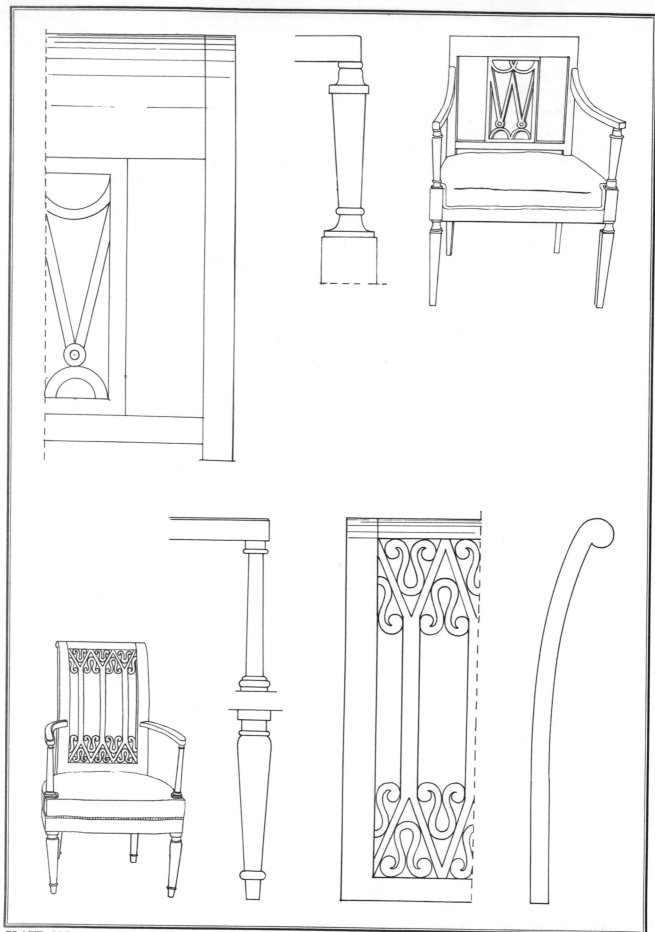

PLATE 302
Charles IV armchairs.

Museum of Decorative Arts and Municipal Museum, Madrid

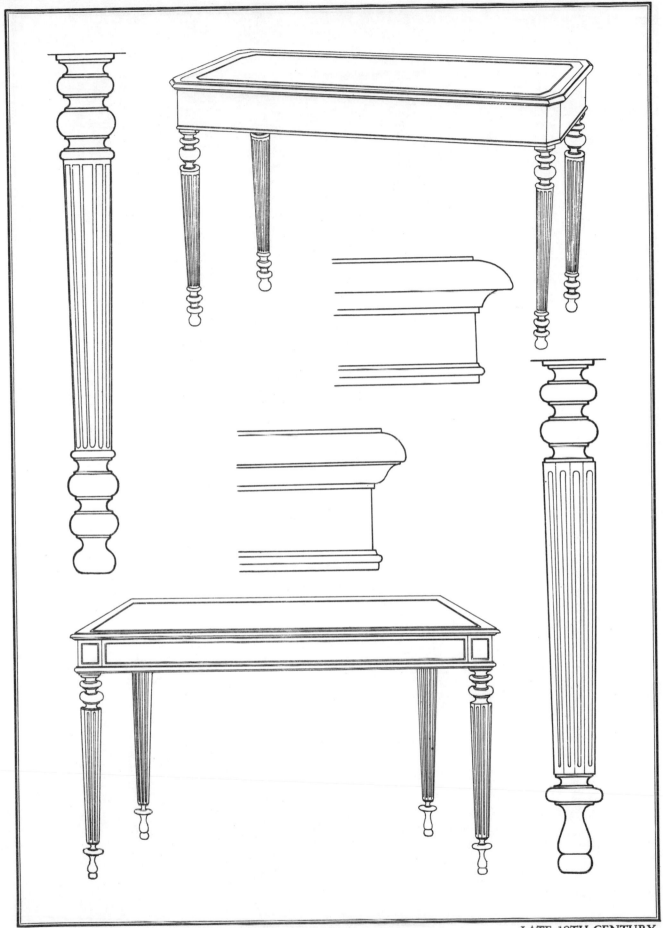

PLATE 303
Louis XVI tables.

LATE 18TH CENTURY

Palace of El Infante Don Alfonso de Orleans, Sanlucar de Barrameda

PLATE 304
Louis XVI writing tables, decorated with marquetry.

LATE 18TH CENTURY

Museum of Decorative Arts, Madrid

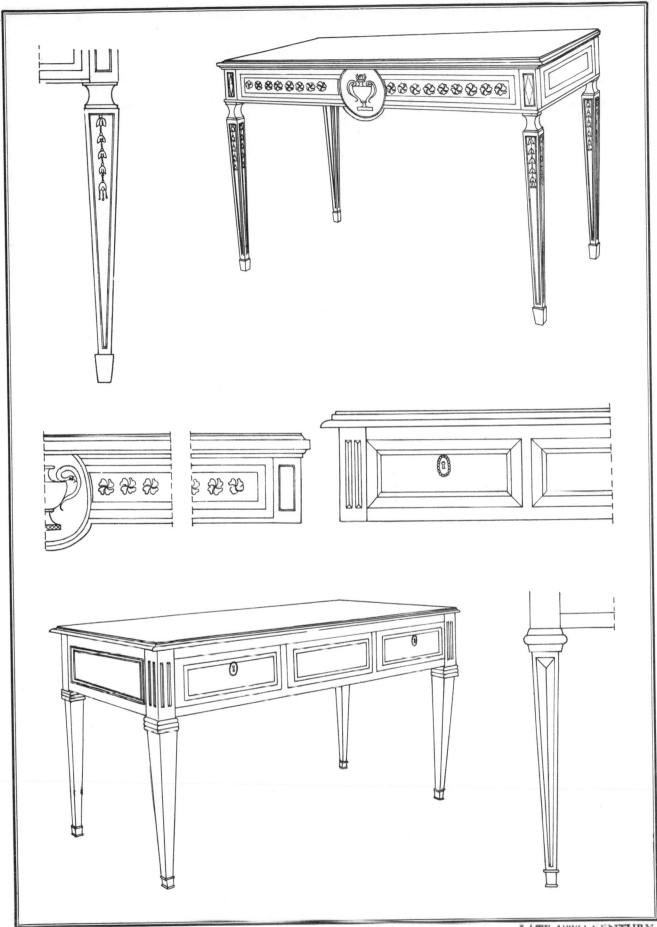

PLATE 305
Louis XVI tables with carved decorations.

Municipal Museum, Madrid

PLATE 306
Charles IV secretary inspired by the English Sheraton style.

LATE 18TH CENTURY

PLATE 307
Catalonian bed, reminiscent of rococo and Louis XVI styles.

311

PLATE 308
Catalonian bed, reminiscent of rococo and Louis XVI styles.

SECOND HALF OF 18TH CENTURY

Cunill collection

PLATE 309
Catalonian bed, reminiscent of rococo and Louis XVI styles.

SECOND HALF OF 18TH CENTURY

Gallifa collection

313

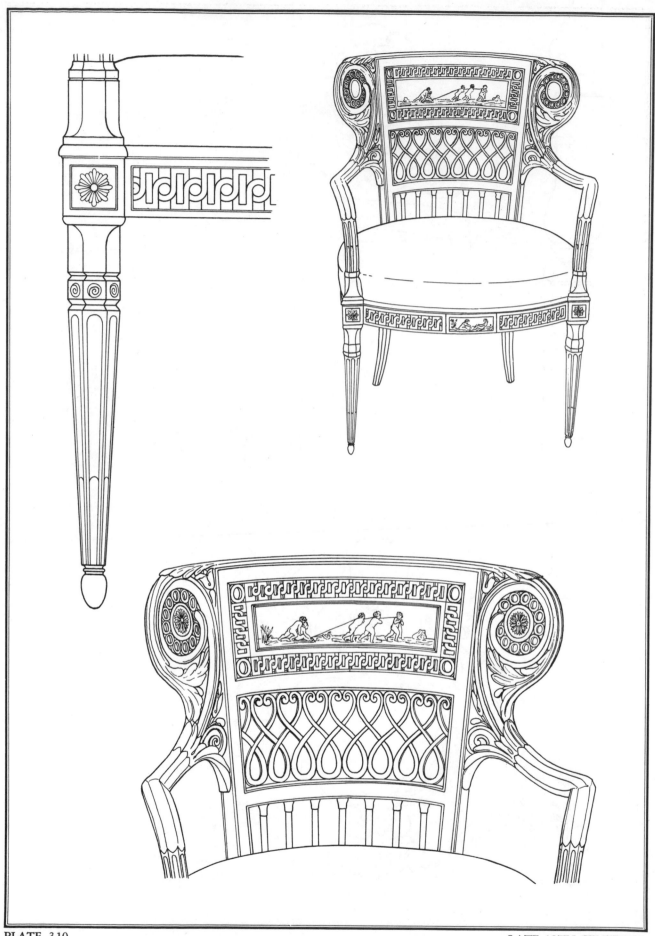

PLATE 310
Charles IV armchair decorated with wood marquetry.

Royal Palace, Madrid

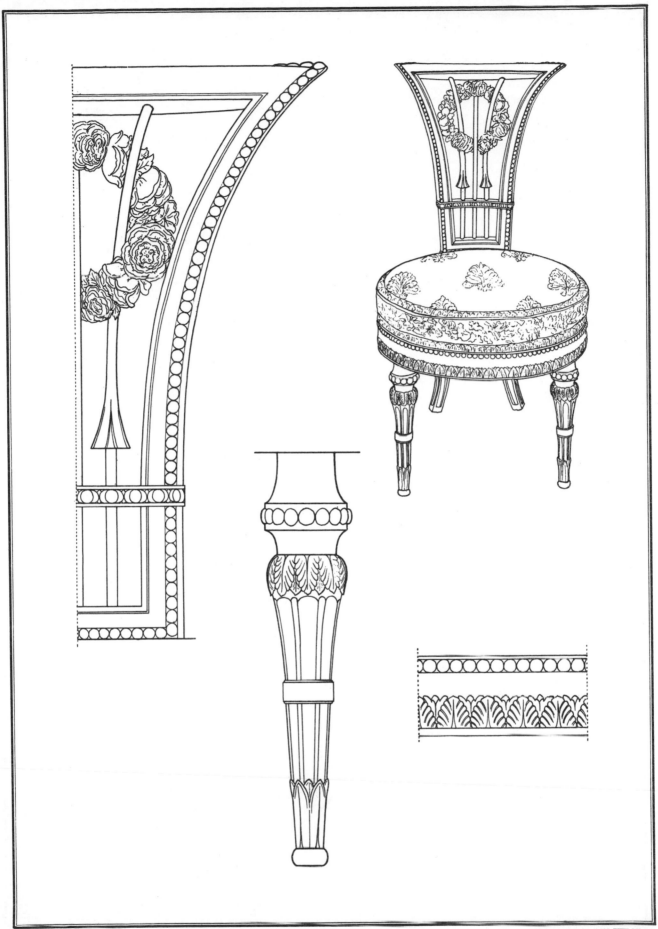

PLATE 311
Charles IV chair trimmed with brushed silk.

Royal Palace, Madrid

PLATE 312
Commode with classical lines, decorated with rococo drawer pulls.

SECOND HALF OF 18TH CENTURY

Gallifa Saborit collection

PLATE 313
Charles IV bed.

Gallifa Sahorit collection

PLATE 314
Louis XV–Louis XVI mirror frame.

Gallifa Saborit collection

PLATE 315
Louis XVI mirror frames.

Romantic Museum and Museum of Decorative Arts, Madrid

PLATE 316
Catalonian bed, reminiscent of rococo and Louis XVI styles.

SECOND HALF OF 18TH CENTURY

Anglada Coll collection

PLATE 317
Catalonian bed, inspired by Louis XVI style.

Babra Arroyos collection

PLATE 318
Charles IV bed.

LATE 18TH CENTURY

Romantic Museum, Madrid

PLATE 319
Charles IV bed.

PLATE 320
Spanish desk, reminiscent of Louis XVI style.

LATE 18TH OR EARLY 19TH CENTURY

PLATE 321
Charles IV chair and small cane sofa.

LATE 18TH OR EARLY 19TH CENTURY

Patrimonio Nacional

PLATE 324
Charles IV cradle with turned balusters.

Mrs. Anton Matheus collection

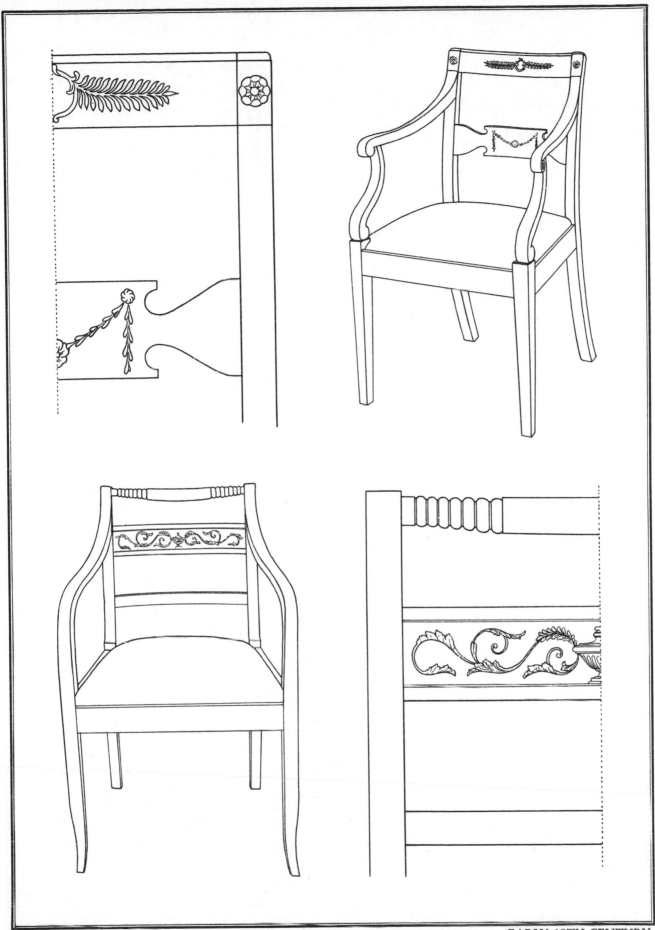

PLATE 325
Charles IV armchairs.

Romantic Museum, Madrid

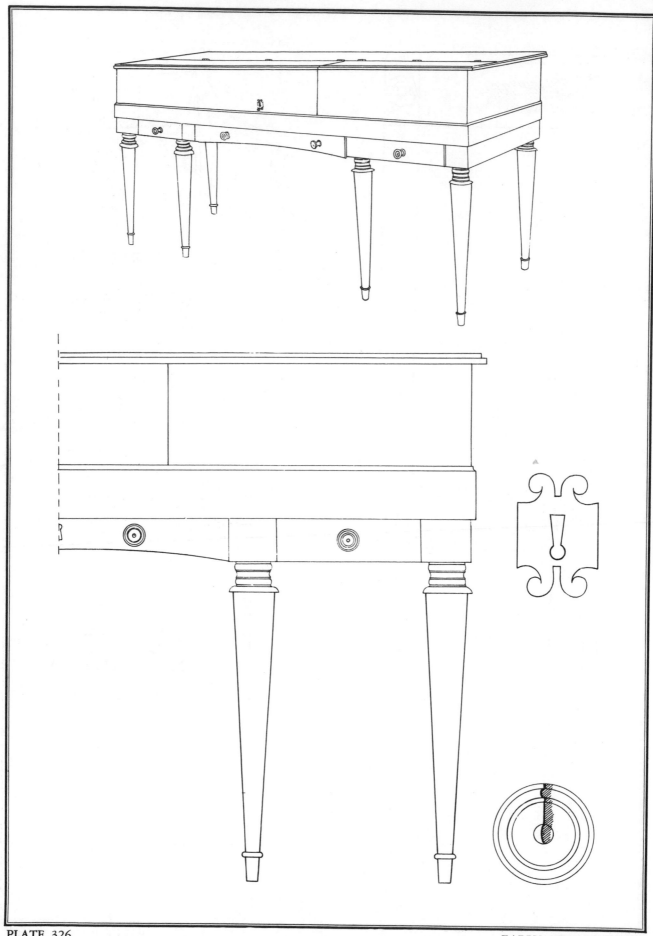

PLATE 326
Louis XVI pianoforte.

Municipal Museum, Madrid

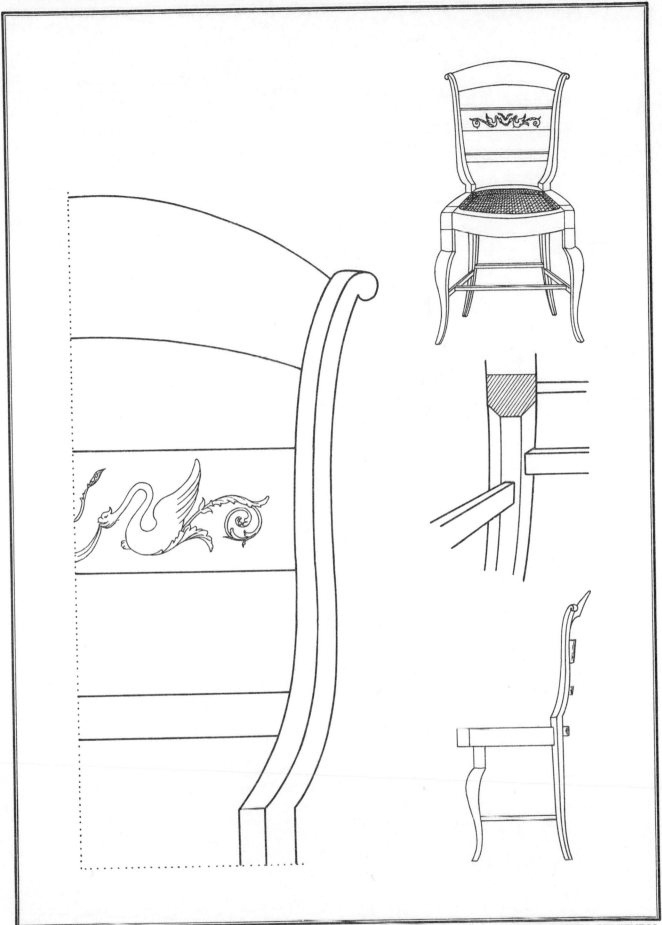

PLATE 327
Spanish cane chair with Empire-style decorative motifs.

EARLY 19TH CENTURY

Antonio Moragas Gallisa collection

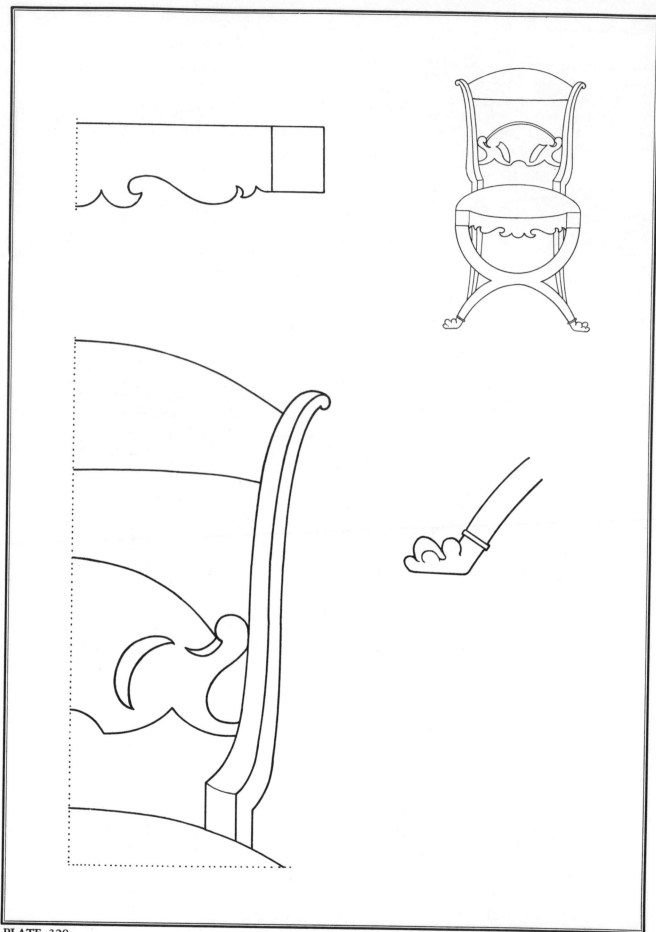

PLATE 328
Empire-style chair.

Rectoret Rigola collection

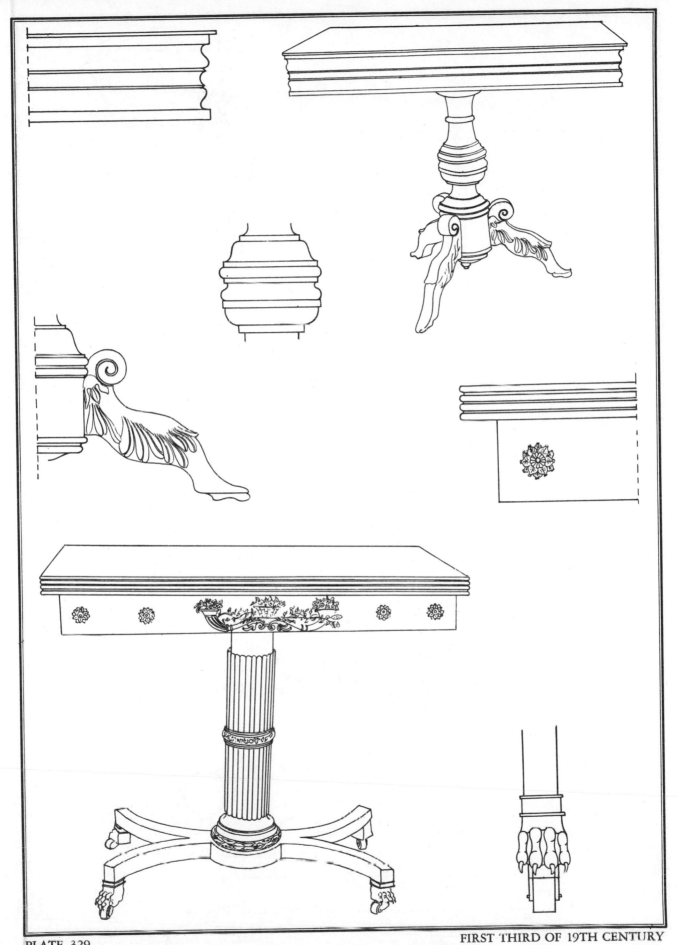

PLATE 329

Pedestal tables. The upper one is Louis Philippe style. The lower one is Empire style.

Romantic Museum and Museum of Decorative Arts, Madrid

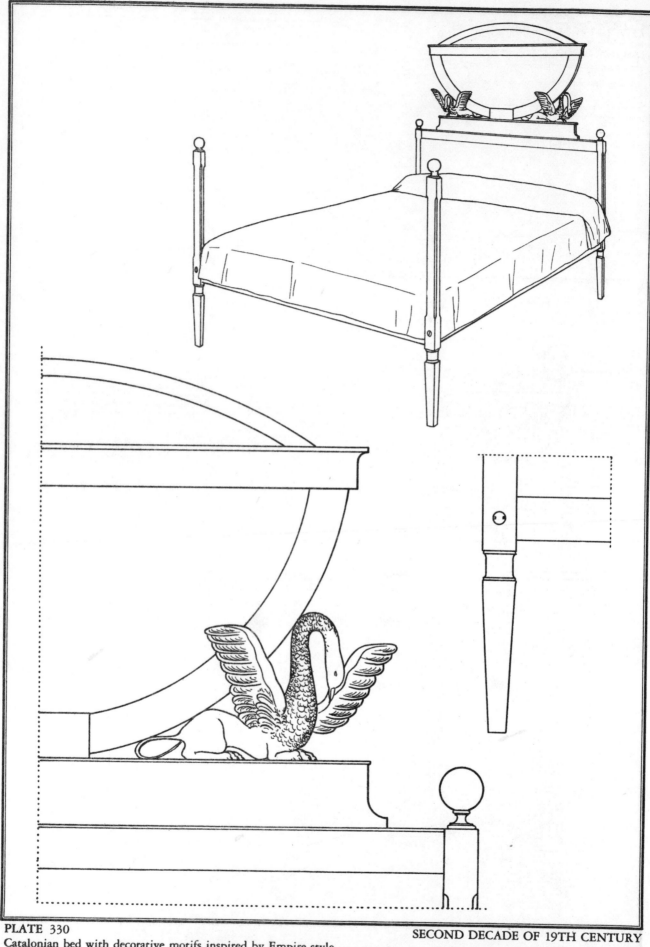

PLATE 330
Catalonian bed with decorative motifs inspired by Empire style.

SECOND DECADE OF 19TH CENTURY

Antonio Moragas Gallisa collection

PLATE 331
Catalonian bed with decorative elements taken from Empire style.

SECOND DECADE OF 19TH CENTURY

Antonio Moragas Gallisa collection

PLATE 332
Catalonian bed with decorative marquetry inspired by Empire style.

SECOND DECADE OF 19TH CENTURY

Louis Armengou Torra collection

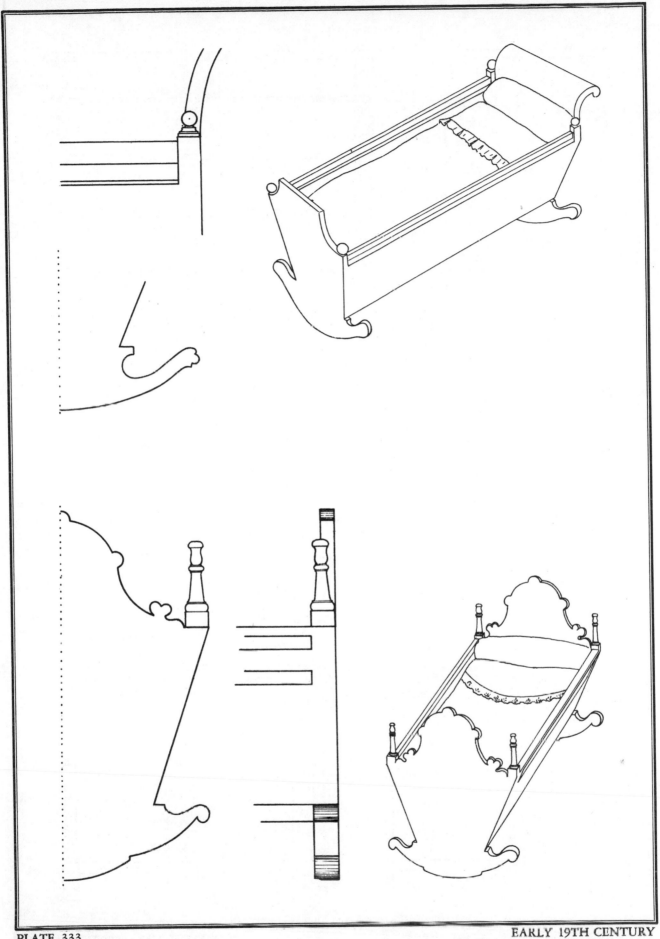

PLATE 333
Catalonian cradles.

Manuel Gallifa Greuzner collection

PLATE 334
SECOND DECADE OF 19TH CENTURY
Mahogany Empire-style commode and dressing table with gilt carved decorations.

Antonio Moragas Gallisa collection

PLATE 335
Mahogany Empire-style dressing table with gilt metal decorations.

Romantic Museum, Madrid

PLATE 336
Door trimming with decorative motifs inspired by Empire style.

Museum of Decorative Arts, Madrid

PLATE 337
English-style commode-bookcase.

Romantic Museum, Madrid

PLATE 338
Restoration-style (Ferdinand VII) sofa.

Romantic Museum, Madrid

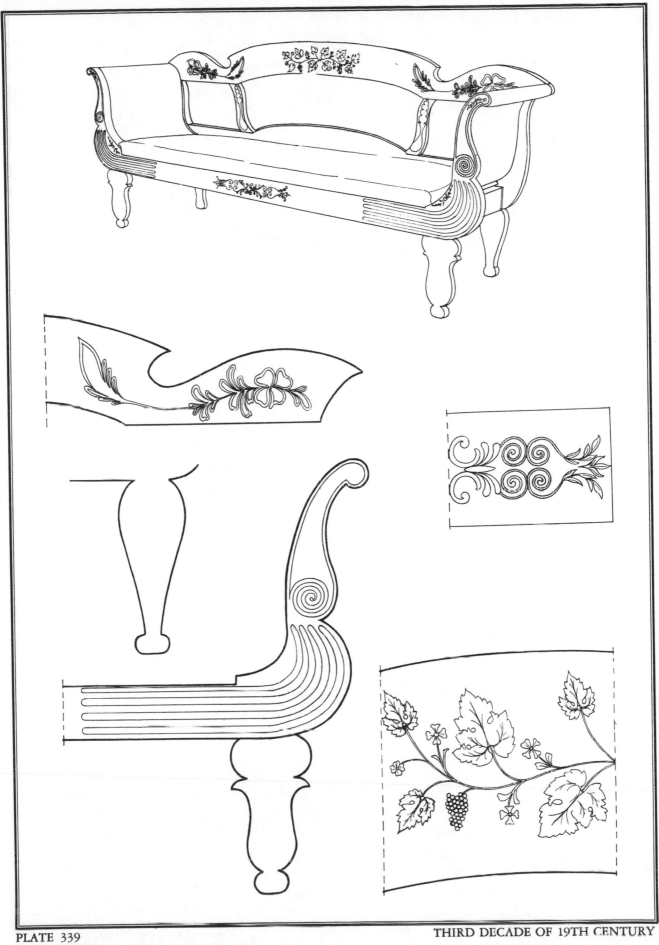

PLATE 339
Ferdinand VII sofa with decorative marquetry.

Romantic Museum, Madrid

PLATE 340
Ferdinand VII sofa with decorative carving and marquetry.

THIRD DECADE OF 19TH CENTURY

Museum of Decorative Arts, Madrid

PLATE 341
Ferdinand VII dressing table with decorative marquetry.

Museum of Decorative Arts, Madrid

345

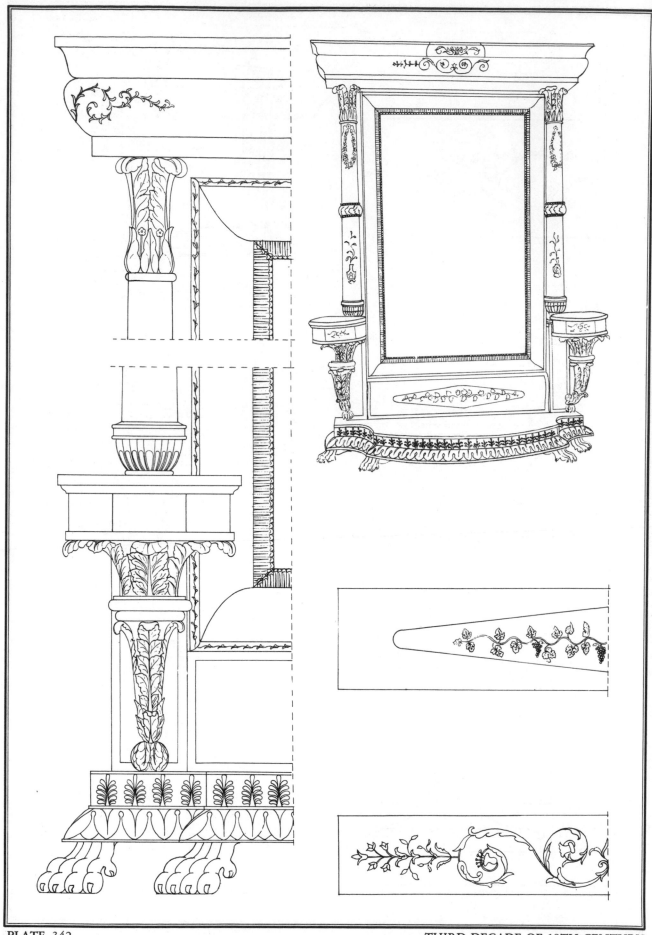

PLATE 342
THIRD DECADE OF 19TH CENTURY

Ferdinand VII dressing-table mirror, decorated with gilt carvings and marquetry.

Museum of Decorative Arts, Madrid

PLATE 343
Louis Philippe console table with turned decorations.

Romantic Museum, Madrid

PLATE 344
Chair and sofa, Isabella style, reminiscent of Louis XV style.

MID-19TH CENTURY

Romantic Museum, Madrid

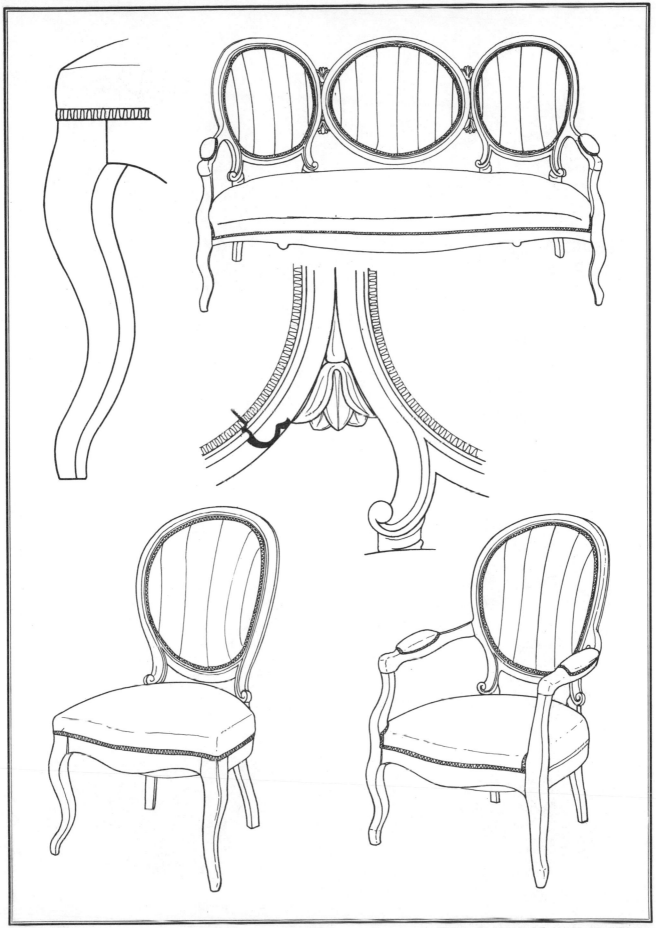

PLATE 345
Sofa, chair and armchair, Isabella style, reminiscent of Louis XVI style.

SECOND HALF OF 19TH CENTURY

Romantic Museum, Madrid

PLATE 346
Gilt carved frames inspired by 18th-century motifs.

Museum of Decorative Arts, Madrid

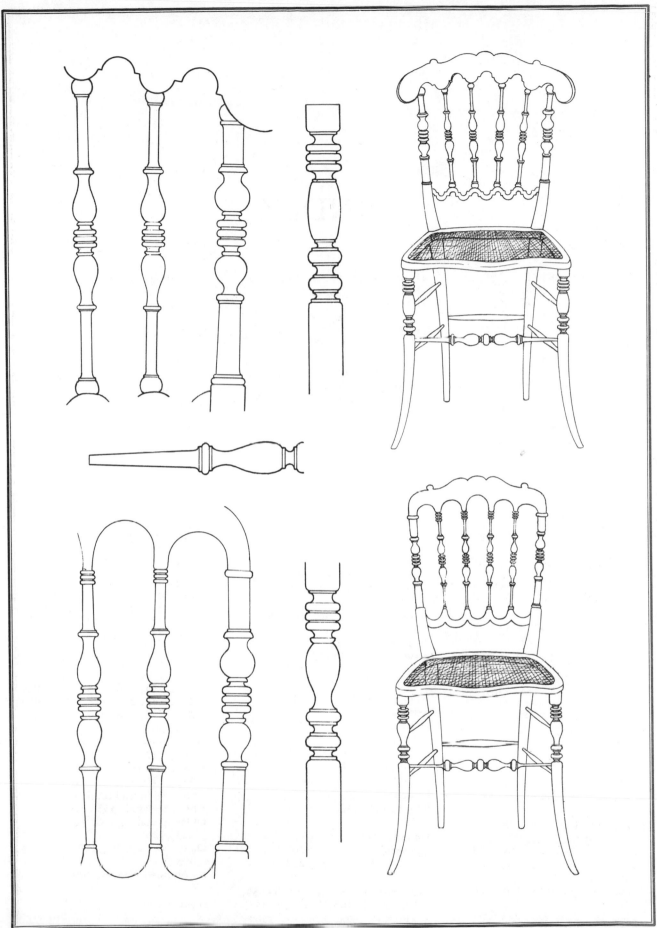

PLATE 347
Chairs from the time of Alfonso XII, inspired by French designs.

Palace of El Infante Don Alfonse de Orleans, Sanlucar de Barrameda

INDEX